# Wicked Western Slope

I0805736

# Wicked Western Slope

## Mayhem, Mischief & Murder in Colorado

D.A. Brockett

THE History PRESS

Published by The History Press
Charleston, SC 29403
www.historypress.net



First published 2012

Manufactured in the United States

ISBN 978.1.60949.570.1

Library of Congress CIP data applied for.

*Notice*: The information in this book is true and complete to the best of our knowledge. It is offered without guarantee on the part of the author or The History Press. The author and The History Press disclaim all liability in connection with the use of this book.

*This book is dedicated to the Museum of Western Colorado's Loyd Files Research Library and to curator Michael Menard. He and his dedicated staff selflessly carry the Western Slope's past into the present and guard it for the future. We should all be thankful.*

# Contents

# Acknowledgements

This book couldn't possibly have been written without the support of my family. Ben and Lily, thank you for sacrificing home-cooked meals, made beds, playtime and loving attention. You're the best! Also, I'd like to thank the following family, friends and colleagues: Steve Henderson, your humor and insight are always sought after and treasured; Garry Brewer, one of my favorite history buds and finder of interesting stories and pictures, some of which were used in this book; Steve and Denise Hight, for insights into Fruita history; Nancy Larson, of the Colorado Prison Museum, for going above and beyond the call of duty to get a picture to me; to Jim Rudnick, Matt Carson, Thelma Liggett, Dorothy Doyle, Darel Paul, Donna Patton, Teri Huff, Susan McCleery's family and especially Michael Menard, curator of the Loyd Files Research Library at the Museum of Western Colorado, I deeply appreciate the pictures you allowed me to use for this book. Thanks, also, to Dr. Robert Kurtzman for answering a medical question for me. Thank you, Priscilla Mangnall and Chris Brown, dear friends and fellow history lovers, for including me in your own history treks over the years. You've helped keep me writing at my computer! Thanks go to my editors, Becky LeJeune and Hilary Parrish of The History Press, for your professional input and care. Lastly, I'd like to thank all who encouraged me to write another book on western Colorado history. Your kind sentiments make all the hard work worthwhile.

# Introduction

Why write a book about early crime on the Western Slope? Certainly not to glory in the gory details. Crime through the ages has shown the trickle-down effect of how the world, as a whole, was doing. For instance, during World War II, there was little crime here, presumably because most of the crooks took their villainous proclivities across the oceans. When the war was over, crime came home, gearing up to ruin Dick and Jane's idyllic lives.

Eras of crime reflect the times. Horse thieving was prolific in the old West, but there was the occasional white-collar crime. Then, a horse was transportation, the ability to work the land and money in the pocket. One can almost understand why people were killed over the loss of a horse back then. Today, a stolen horse is a rare thing, and murder over it is even rarer. But in a world of exploding information and the Internet, white-collar crimes are at tsunami proportions.

The first newspaper in town, the *Grand Junction News*, meticulously reported on every little jot and tittle. However, where early crime was concerned, its editors either played it down or reprimanded the miscreants like outraged mothers. Not that they were soft on criminals or overly judgmental. They were trying to grow the valley, and how would it look to the outside world if the area was flush with iniquity or didn't take a stand for propriety?

Much credit for weathering early Western Slope life goes to the *News*. There was no denying the harsh existence, and to withstand the disappointments and dismay, a certain amount of humor was needed. Edwin Price and D.P. Kingsley doled out the news in carefully modulated columns. They were in the unique position of impacting a town's future with the truth while discouraging the weary masses from leaving. Humor was the key. If they could banter about the buffoonery, then the readers could, too. It worked, and a strong communal bond was woven throughout the valley.

This book reflects the different decades of an emerging metropolis. You'll find some quoted colloquial terms offensive, but they've been included to show how we, as a society, have grown regarding prejudicial behaviors. Like a modern police blotter, these stories have tragedy, murder, rape and atrocities of every ilk. Some take a cue from the *News* and celebrate the funny side of seriousness—for, as Roman Gary wrote, "Humor is an affirmation of dignity, a declaration of man's superiority to all that befalls him." Most importantly, you'll understand how the determination, wisdom, dedication, strength and vision that a tenacious group of people embraced created a successful society, in spite of the dark times.

# *Chapter 1*
# I Fought the Law and...

## Hotheads, Inc.

Not much went on in the way of crime during the inaugural year of Grand Junction. Cabin raising, business building and surviving the elements were at the top of the to-do list. Important businesses were established first. A bank, livery, grocery store and plenty of saloons dotted the sagebrush corridor dubbed "Hoodoo Avenue." Emma Thompson's log cabin saloon was always busy, day and night. The first recorded shooting in town took place there on Thursday, November 10, 1882.

Earlier in the week, on election night, an earthquake had rocked the town and rattled the nerves of residents. By Thursday night, tempers were short, and two men—Mike Dunn, a young railroader who'd been sacked earlier in the week, and a gambler named "Broken-Nose" Sims—got into it. Sims pulled out his gun and shot at Dunn's retreating body as he exited the back door. The gambler missed, but panic ensued in the smoky room.

As people stumbled around, Kitty Sheedy, a prostitute, fell and broke her arm. When Marshal Jim Davis barreled in to see what in tarnation was going on, the crowd pointed at the back door and shouted, "Arrest that man, for God's sake!"

Davis skimmed out the back door and saw Dunn running down the alley. He hollered for the man to stop, but he was too scared and kept his pace. Davis opened fire, and Dunn slammed to the ground, a bullet in his back. The doctor was called for, and he transferred Dunn to the nearby hospital at the southeast corner of Second and Colorado. Not to leave any loose ends,

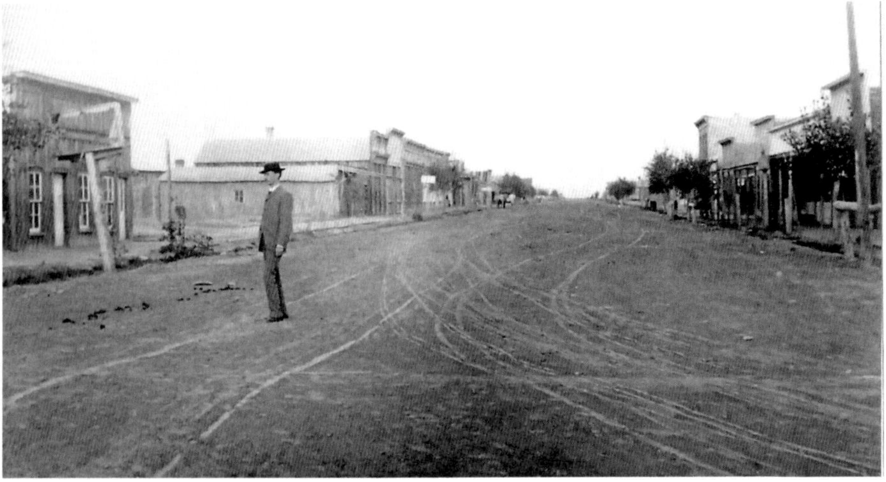

One block south of Main Street, Colorado Avenue was dubbed "Hoodoo Avenue" for its crime element. This photo was taken in 1882 and was the original business section. As saloons and brothels flourished, especially in the early years, reputable businesses happily migrated to Main Street when it began to be developed. At this corner, the man's back is facing Emma Thompson's Saloon. *Courtesy of Loyd Files Research Library.*

Sims was secured in jail to await a preliminary trial. It was only then that Marshal Jim Davis turned himself over to Deputy Sheriff Brown.

Though the *Grand Junction News* gave no indication, the town was in an uproar over the shooting. When Dunn died four days later, several men from Company F, the local militia, mustered and planned to teach Davis a lesson. They were up in arms that the lawman, a musician, was fiddling at a dance hall rather than showing proper grief. One soldier sent Davis a drawing of him with a rope around his neck, alongside a threatening note. Courage faltered, and the soldiers went home before they made good on their threat.

Following Davis was another hothead officer. Marshal Tim Crowley shot a black man as he begged for his life. George Lewis died the next morning. Crowley turned himself in, as was the custom, but was quickly exonerated by a jury.

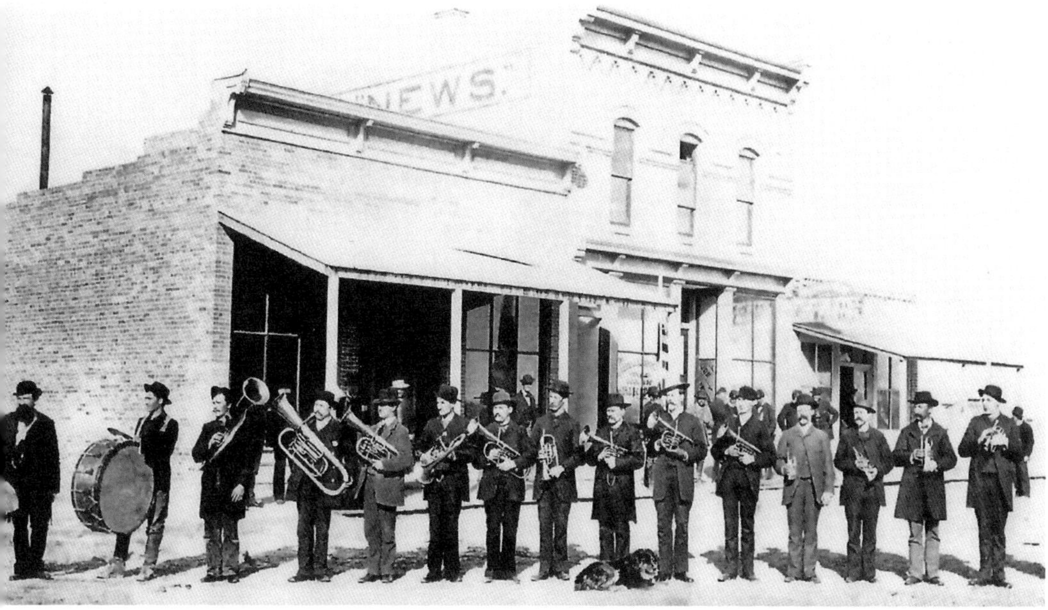


Marshal Tim Crowley and Mayor A.A. Miller both belonged to the first cornet band of Grand Junction. This 1883 photo was taken in front of the second *News* office, located on the north side of Main between Fifth and Sixth Streets. Crowley, who played second E flat tuba, is the fourth man from the left. Mayor Miller stands behind the dog and played second alto. *Courtesy of Loyd Files Research Library.*

Townsfolk weren't so forgiving. Since its inception, Crowley had played with the Grand Junction Cornet Band, and when he tried to rejoin them after he got out of jail, he was blackballed. He got into trouble several times over the following years, and it's told he eventually went crazy and died at the Pueblo Insane Asylum.

In October 1907, a railroad depot officer and sheriff's deputy, Frank Mahaney, wrestled with a black man named Wade Johnson at the tracks. Mahaney was commissioned to stop hobos from hitching rides on the train

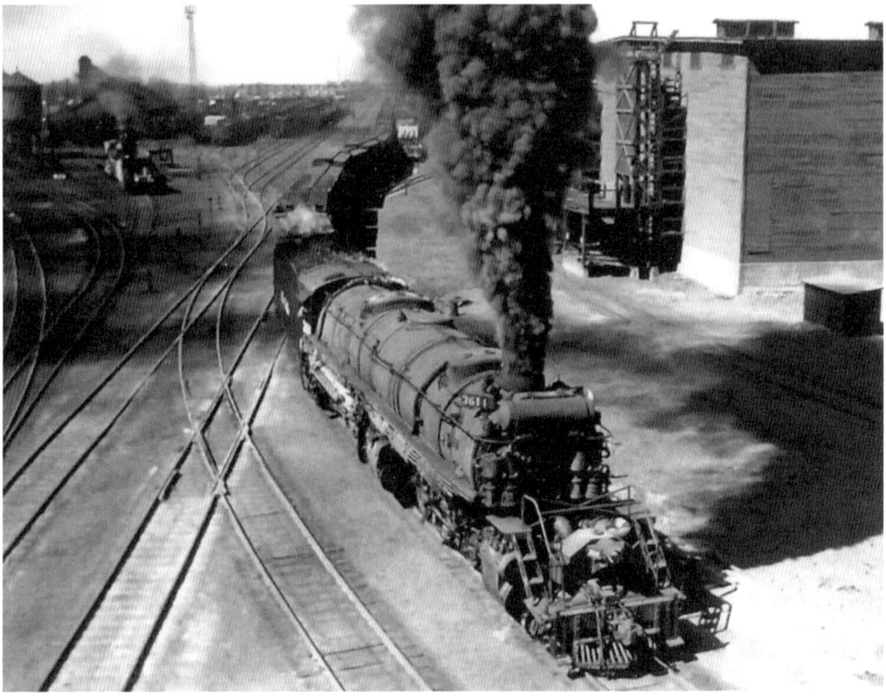

In 1882, the Denver & Rio Grande Railroad had built its rails to Grand Junction, transforming it into a company town overnight. Boosters and businesses were ecstatic, as area growth exploded. A roundhouse, icehouses, an array of tracks and its beautiful depot bustled with workers, visitors, hobos and the occasional crook. *Courtesy of Loyd Files Research Library.*

cars. He claimed that he saw Johnson "stealthily" trying to board the Denver & Rio Grande No. 6 and that he'd pulled the man off and confronted him. Next, he claimed, he was fighting for his life.

Mahaney said he fired three bullets into Johnson, "in self defense," when the man pulled a gun. Dr. Thadd Parker was called to the scene and found the dead man perforated with three gunshot wounds. One was lodged in the upper right side of his head, one in the right side of his neck and another four inches below his left nipple.

An inquest was quickly assembled at the Krohn Funeral Parlor on Main Street. Coroner H.S. Day kept it private but allowed a *Daily Sentinel* reporter in. Mahaney had turned himself in to Sheriff Schrader and sat in the county jail. As the inquest began, a great crowd milled outside Krohn's discussing the details. A majority of them were railroad men who didn't like Mahaney. They said they'd refuse to move any trains if the man was found not guilty. They felt the shooting wasn't "fully justified."

Mahaney wasn't new to inquests. He'd killed a poacher on the Grand Mesa several years prior, for which he was pardoned. He got into trouble again when, in 1906, he arrested an upstanding citizen at the depot for not disclosing his railroad ticket. At that moment, there was a $10,000 false arrest suit pending. These events didn't make Mahaney very popular.

The night of the murder, Minnie Spencer visited the morgue and identified the remains as Wade Johnson from Montrose. She said he'd been with her all afternoon and had left to go downtown "for a little while." It appeared that he was ditching the woman, the coroner told her. Instead of hanging about, he'd gone directly to the depot to flip a ride out of town. Miss Spencer was "greatly grieved."

There was no doubt that Johnson had prepared for a journey. He wore two suits of clothing, a vest, two coats and two pairs of trousers. In his pockets were a box of cocaine, a half-empty flask of whiskey, a letter addressed to him from Montrose and a pair of gloves. He had no money on him. The gun he allegedly had was found a ways from his body, lying near some railroad tracks. Several of Johnson's friends contended that the gun was placed there after the shooting.

The members of the inquest jury found they didn't have enough evidence to decide one way or the other and deemed Mahaney "neither justified nor censured" regarding the killing.

The *Sentinel*'s October 11, 1907 headline announced the sensational arrest of Frank Mahaney after "well-known local colored man" T.P. Langdon swore out an arrest. The charge was "malicious and willful murder" of Johnson. The entire African American community was behind him.

Mahaney remained in the county jail until his preliminary hearing, which took place in the October session of district court. Justice of the Peace J.P. Sweney presided over the preliminary hearing on October 14 to a packed house. The rumor was that the prosecution had new evidence against Mahaney, and despite the death of the original attorney hired, Thomas C. Brown, there was still hope that Mahaney would get his due. The outcome wasn't surprising, as little new evidence was supplied. Mahaney "was discharged."

Over the months, the newspaper had stood in the guilty gallery, but now, the *Sentinel* stated, "few people believed that he was guilty of murder."

It was said that City Officer Andy L. Halligan could handle a parade almost single-handedly, due to his large size. Yet he was the smallest of several policemen in his family. One Saturday in 1908, his large hands got him into trouble.

On duty as a special officer at the fairgrounds near today's St. Mary's Hospital, he struck W.A. Van Buren. Van Buren said it was without cause but did concede that he'd had a few drinks and had called Halligan "a big dub." Halligan admitted that he'd "tapped" Van Buren with his open hand. Halligan was found not guilty.

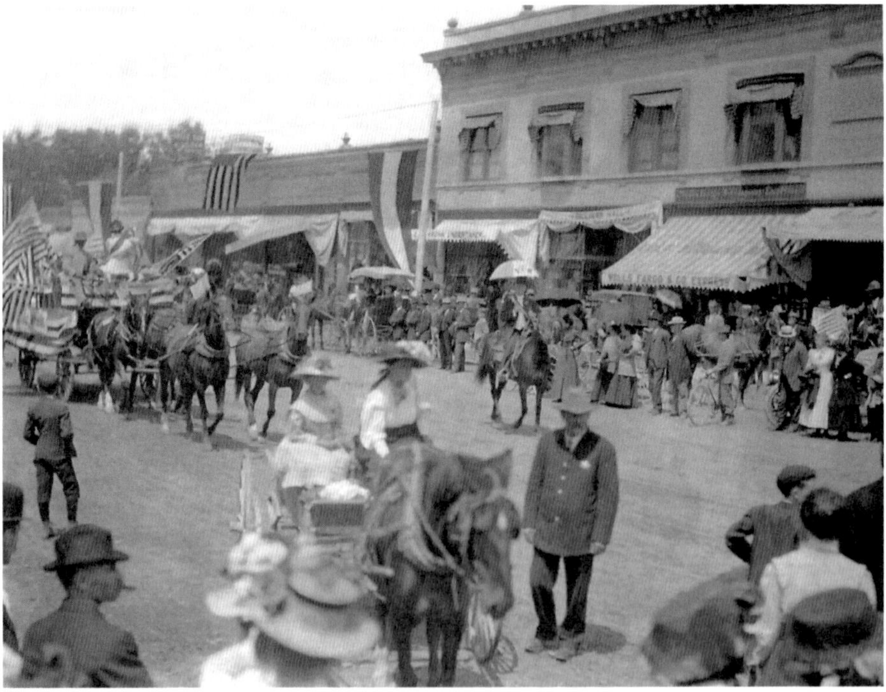

Main Street often had parades in the early years, mostly military related, as the Grand Valley Guards' Company F and the Grand Army of the Republic were a presence on the Western Slope. This photo was possibly taken in 1890. Lawman Andy Halligan kept the spectators in check, here at the corner of Fourth and Main. E.A. Krohn's Undertaking, Wells Fargo Express and a billiards hall are seen in the background. *Courtesy of Loyd Files Research Library.*

The *Grand Junction News* of January 4, 1890, reported:

> *On Tuesday evening Joseph Bresler in a partially intoxicated condition, took supper at the "Saddle-Rock" restaurant, and then refused to pay for it. Marshall Thomas Butts was near at hand and was requested by Mr. Graff, the proprietor of the restaurant, to arrest Bresler. Bresler objected and struck an attitude of determination to fight. Mr. Butts struck him two or three slight blows with his revolver which, at the last blow, was discharged, the ball entering the right side of Bresler's head and passing around the scalp, lodged in such a position that the surgeons say it would cause instant death to remove it. Bresler's condition is somewhat critical. Officer Butts gave himself up to the sheriff, but the general sentiment seems to attach no blame to him.*

Reported in January 25's paper: "The preliminary hearing for Marshal Butts was held. Mr. Bresler has recovered from his wound, and as the shooting appeared to be purely accidental, Mr. Butts was discharged. The public is pleased."

## Horse Thieves' Canon

Considering how tough pioneers had to be in order to wrangle the land into something livable, tenacity was a key ingredient of the pioneer soul. Early law enforcers had their challenges, too, as crime happened across the Western Slope. Dedication and patience were as important as a six-shooter and a strong horse. Horses were so important to the cultivation of the land that to steal one was serious business.

In late 1888, a gang of horse thieves roamed the Western Slope and eastern Utah, successfully stealing hundreds of horses. The *News* was getting a bit miffed at the law's bumbling attempts to capture the miscreants. Finally, a February 1889 jaunt by Sheriff Cramer and Barney Kennedy rooted out their camp near Moab, Utah. Young Pavey and his partners, Derickson and Goodwin, were sighted from a ledge of rocks overhanging their hiding place.

Derickson spotted the officers and "snapped his six-shooter at the sheriff." The sheriff retaliated by sending a couple of bullets through the thief's bedclothes. Goodwin and Derickson got away, "owing to the roughness of the country," but Pavey was caught, along with the stolen horses. Pavey was put in county jail, under a $2,000 bond, to await trial. The other two were captured shortly after.

Two weeks later, the *News* reported a horse-thieving foible that almost ended in the death of Barney Kennedy. A couple of suspicious-looking fellows were "loafing" outside the Senate Saloon one evening. Hitched to a post in front of the saloon was Mr. McCabe's horse. Sheriff Cramer and Marshal Kennedy decided to check out the men.

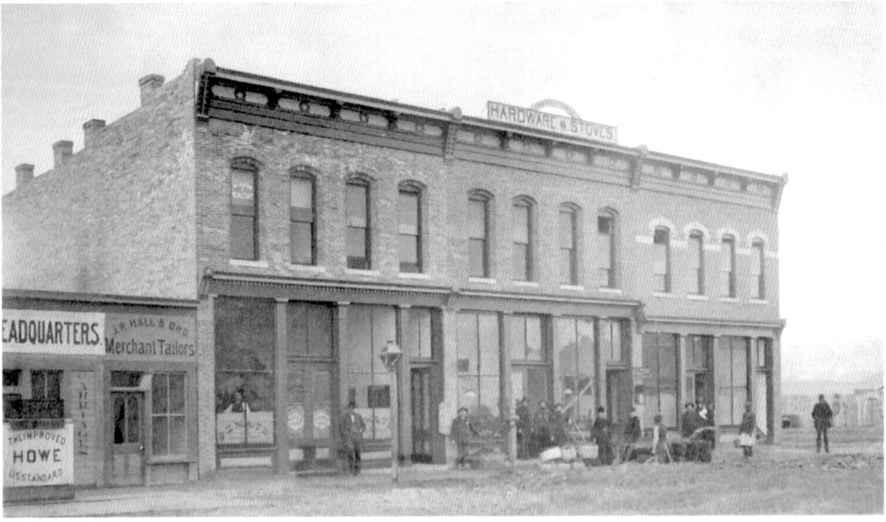


The Senate Saloon opened in the new business block near the southeast corner of Main and Fourth Streets in 1884. It would remain in business until 1955, weathering Prohibition by selling soft drinks. Though it had several different owners, James Purcell ran it the longest. Standing beside the second entrance from the left is Marshal Tim Crowley, wearing a badge. This building still stands. *Courtesy of Loyd Files Research Library.*

Thinking they might have some horses in town, the lawmen scanned Colorado Avenue, where the majority of liveries were located. The two separated at Third Street. Cramer headed east toward Hammond's stables, and Kennedy headed west toward Prairie's. Near Fourth Street, Kennedy noticed that McCabe's saddled horse was now hitched to a post at J.T. Howard's stable. As he approached the little attached cabin, he heard low voices. Kennedy listened for a few minutes and concluded they were the suspicious men and that they must have stolen McCabe's horse.

The reason for Kennedy's next actions are unclear, but standing in front of the door, he lit a match and held it inside a crack. It was instantly knocked out of his hand. Stepping back a bit, he shot through the crack but missed his target. One of the fellows dashed for the open window at the rear of the cabin, but Kennedy ran to meet him. The thief was out the window and on the run when Kennedy shot at him. He fell once but got up and disappeared into the darkness. Kennedy sprang to the front of the cabin to see about the other man. Just as he reached it, a bullet sailed through the door from inside, barely missing Kennedy. By this time, Sheriff Cramer had reached the scene, and several more shots were exchanged.

Maybe it was all that gun smoke clouding the law's eyes, but both horse thieves got away. The *News* wrote, "It was a narrow escape for the fellows, and it is a wonder they were not wounded."

## The Circus Grandstands

Local lawmen took their jobs seriously, even with the small crimes. An early case in point was when the circus came to town. Everyone was excited when Sanger & Lent's "combination" pulled in. They had knife-throwers, trained dogs, monkeys, birds and two vampires, as well as Professor Madden, the magician. A parade usually always led the festivities, but not on May 20, 1893. Someone got mad that the circus hadn't paid a street performance fee for its parade and made a fuss about it.

The circus had set up its tents just outside of town, near the Carpenters' beautiful home, Fairlawn. This way, it would bypass any additional fees. All was well until the circus lined up for the usual street parade on Main Street. The *News* wrote: "The horses were bedecked with gay plumage, the fool-maker was painted up and dressed to the queen's taste, and the baby elephant ordered to the rear."

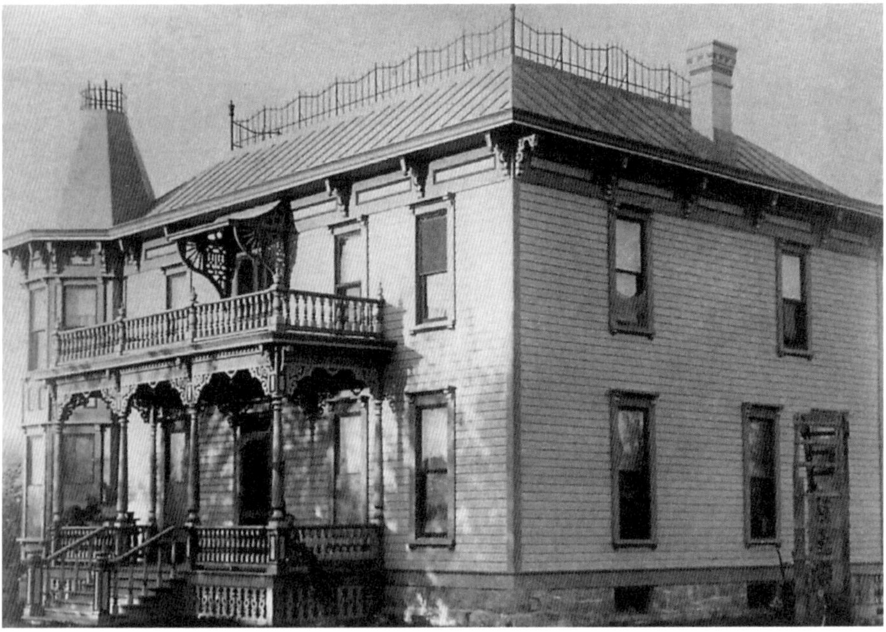

William T. Carpenter had Fairlawn built in the 1880s. William was a banker and booster and one of the main movers for the Little Book Cliff Railway. Etta, his wife, brought music and culture to the Western Slope, and their daughter, Susan, made a name for herself as a singer. Fairlawn was the site of many fun evenings, but when the silver market crash nearly shut the bank's doors in 1892, the Carpenters moved away. Fairlawn became a hotel and then a sanitarium before being torn down for Gay Johnson's Restaurant. *Courtesy of the Susan McCleery family.*

The band began to play "Annie Rooney," and the order was given to proceed. The circus workers felt rather full of themselves for getting one over on the city officials.

Barely had the last strains of the trumpet bleated away when City Marshal Ketchum ordered the procession to cease. The bugler blustered and argued and was promptly arrested. The next officer in charge took Ketchum's countenance to heart and called an about face, but not before shouting the times of the performances. He, too, was arrested. The whole procession marched back to the tents, defeated.

A hearing before Justice Sweney garnered a two-dollar fine for each man, as well as costs. The circus won in the end, with public opinion favoring its side. The performances were given and drew great crowds.

## Ketchum Catches 'Im

In the early 1890s, the town was overrun with hobos and dogs. Quite a few citizens had been bitten by vicious canines, and there was an outcry for something to be done. An ordinance had been issued to dog owners to license and curb their dogs. The fine for breaking this law was heavy—death. Not for the owners, of course, but for their pets.

City Marshal Ketchum took guff from no one, and a bad attitude landed C.W. Rundle behind bars. At the packed trial, Ketchum testified that he had frequently seen Rundle's dog running or lying on the streets and that he was dangerous. He stated that on this particular morning, the dog had followed Rundle's wagon to town and was lying on the street. Ketchum attempted to snare the dog, but his owner knocked the snare away, saying the dog was with him. Rundle was arrested, and at the trial, the jury retired for five minutes before finding Rundle guilty.

## Bedwell Gets By

The law has never been equal, even if democratic hearts would like to think so. Reading the newspapers of the time, one can see inequities in the divvying up of justice. Still, as in raising children, what is good for one may not be the best approach for another.

In the case of H.G. Bedwell, accused of attempted murder on J.A. McLeun, the law appears to have been lenient. Bedwell owned a livery on Colorado Avenue and was a horse breeder and racer. As a matter of fact, he was the best one around. This may have been the seed that started a bitter rift between him and McLeun that culminated in an almost deadly scrap on Christmas Eve 1904. Perhaps if Bedwell had been home with his family instead of drinking at the Abbey Saloon, things would have turned out differently. Instead, Bedwell opened a severe gash on McLeun's left cheek with a knife. McLeun staggered home and remained there for a week recuperating. His anger simmered until he finally filed a complaint against Bedwell on New Year's Eve. Bedwell was taken to jail.

That was a hard day for him. He'd lost his prize horse, Thornbud, the night before he was arrested. Thornbud was the best blooded horse around and was in the top ten in the nation.

No other details made it into the newspapers until March 25, 1905, when the *News* relayed the district court proceedings. Whether soft hearts prevailed

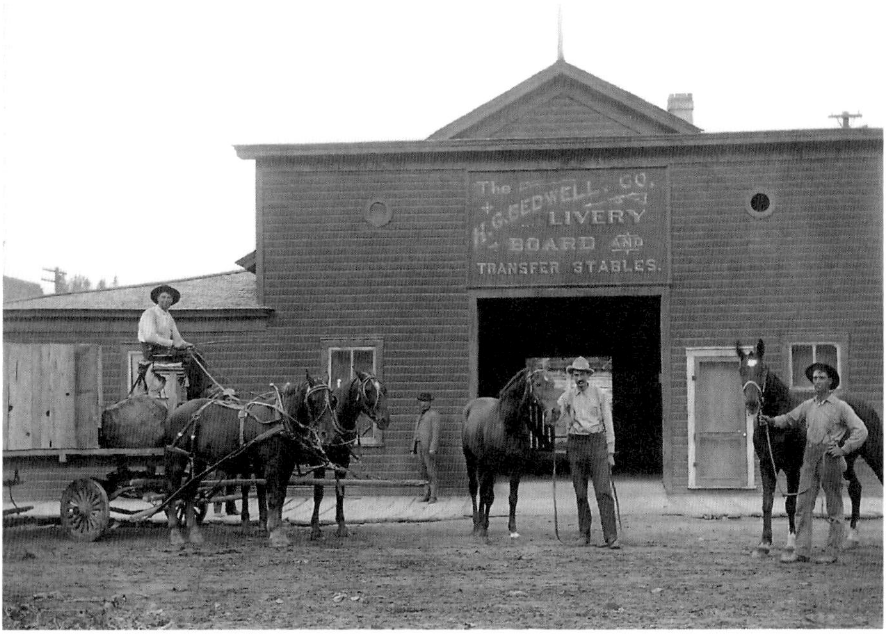


Harvey Guy "Hard Guy" Bedwell was an early livery owner. His stables were located on the northwest corner of Colorado Avenue and Third Street, just a couple of doors down from the infamous 240. Raised by a single mother during the Gold Rush days, he toughened up quickly. He learned excellent horsemanship skills while a cowboy in Oregon and used those skills to train many racehorses, including the first Triple Crown winner, Sir Barton. *Courtesy of Loyd Files Research Library.*

due to Bedwell's loss of Thornbud or Bedwell's standing in the community, after he pleaded guilty, he was simply fined for his indiscretion. He went on to be inducted into the National Museum of Racing and Hall of Fame after he trained the first Triple Crown winner, Sir Barton.

## Emma Does Not

It's sad to say, but Emma Nelson didn't get the same consideration as Bedwell. A woman of "easy virtue," she lived on Ute Avenue near the red-light district. In September 1889, she went to the police and filed a theft report. Someone had entered a window of her house and stolen a bed cover, a toilette set and $125 worth of jewelry.

Several thefts around town had recently occurred, so her story probably wasn't fabricated, but the police gave little attention to her plight. Undeterred, she took matters into her own hands. The *News* reported on September 21, "The fair damsel tackled a fellow on the street whom she saw carrying a quilt and held him up at the point of a gun, but he proved to be the wrong fellow."

A week later, Emma decided to try a more benign approach. She posted an ad in the *News* on October 5, 1889: "Reward: $20 will be paid for the return of rings (stolen) one amethyst, two emeralds and one opal, one diamond, one garnet and pearl, taken from Emma Nelson's residence, on Ute Avenue near depot."

## A Beloved—and Smart—Sheriff

Not all law enforcement officers were inept or quick draws, although Police Chief Frank Clifton accidentally shooting himself while changing his tire begs to challenge that perception. The good chief had leaned over to deal with the tire when his gun fell out of its holster. It hit the pavement and discharged a bullet, severing an artery in his arm. He survived but wasn't chief for long.

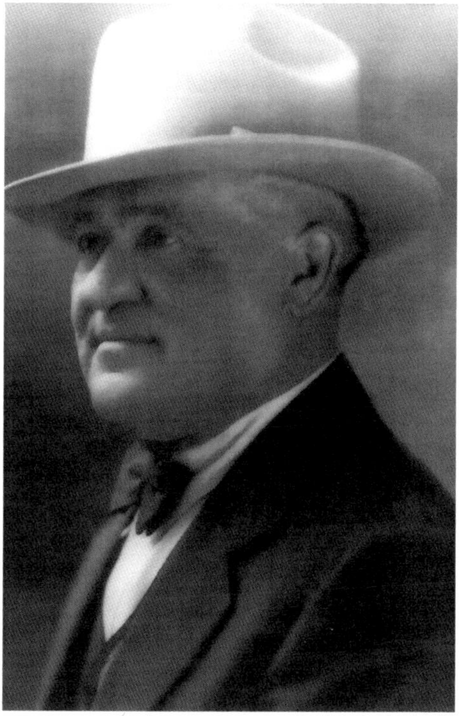

Sheriff Charles "Charley" Lumley was a consummate politician, but it was because he loved his job. Political ads stated, "Charles Lumley loves wayward boys." Today, that would raise some eyebrows, but everyone knew Charley wanted the best for those whose feet were on the wrong path. He died in office of an illness. His funeral was probably one of the largest the area had ever seen. *Courtesy of Teri Huff, granddaughter of Sheriff Lumley.*

Charles S. Lumley, sheriff from 1929 to 1941, when he died in office, was beloved by everyone, including his prisoners. He had a warm, fatherly way about him, and even when bringing in a crook, he gave him a pep talk and encouraged him to get his life straight. He often received letters of thanks from penitentiary inmates and from the parents of those who'd turned their lives around because of his concern.

Criminals handled themselves differently around Charley. His wife, Rose, was fond of telling this story: One evening, she was at the county jail (located at the time on the south side of White Avenue, between Fifth and Sixth Streets), where she and Charley lived on the first floor. There came a knock at the jail door, and Rose answered it. She smiled at the well-known citizen standing there, but it slipped away when he quietly explained he'd just shot someone at a card game. Rather than put the sheriff out on a search, he would save him the trouble and turn himself in. While Rose waited, a bit uncomfortably, for her husband to arrive, the man sat patiently in a nearby chair with his hands on his knees.

Charley's gentle persuasiveness brought in a member of the notorious Fleagle Gang. Two years prior, the gang had pulled off a deadly bank robbery in Lamar, Colorado, killing the bank president and his son at the scene. Several other murders occurred on their rampage across the Midwest.

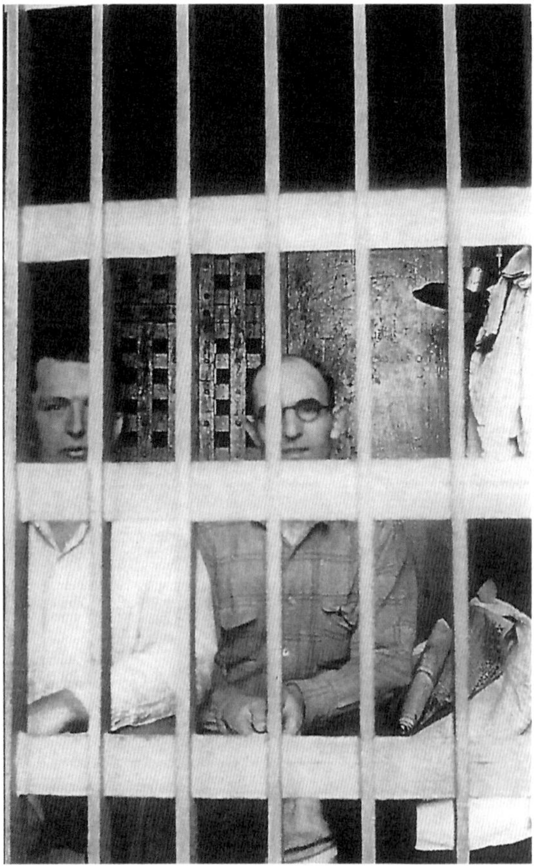

George Abshire, aka Bill Messick, member of the deadly Fleagle Gang, was captured by Sheriff Lumley in Grand Junction. On May 23, 1928, he, Ralph and Jake Fleagle and Howard Royston robbed the First National Bank in Lamar, Colorado. It was a messy affair that left the bank president, A.N. Parrish, dead, as well as his son, Jaddo. Howard Roystun was injured when Parrish shot him in the jaw. They took almost $250,000 in monies and escaped with hostages. They later coldheartedly killed the doctor who helped patch up Royston. *Courtesy of Teri Huff.*

In 1930, Charley was going through a stack of mug shots and recognized one immediately. Fleagle Gang member George Abshier was alive and living well in Grand Junction. But Charley knew him as a bootlegger named Bill Messick. Messick lived at the McAlma rooming house on Rood Avenue.

Charley drove downtown, keeping an eye out for Messick, and finally spotted him on Main Street, sitting in his brand-new car with his girlfriend. He approached the murderer and pleasantly informed Bill he needed him down at the station. Messick asked, "Is it about that bootleg deal?" and Charley nodded. Messick climbed into the sheriff's car and went to the jail. After he was locked up, he learned the jig was up. Later, when the sheriff searched the car, he found a loaded gun strapped under the steering wheel.

Abshier/Messick was hanged in Canon City on July 18, 1930.

# *Chapter 2*
# Moxie Posses

## An Ousting We Will Go

On August 25, 1883, the *Grand Junction News* published an impassioned editorial entitled "Law or Violence?" It recounted a very tense week centering on a dangerous local movement to forcibly remove the Chinese population. The few who lived there were engaged in small laundries and quietly contributing to the growth of the town. That was fine, but when opium dens cropped up, animosity did too. Even worse, some of the elite citizens patronized the dens. The Chinese were blamed for eroding the fine fabric of the town.

The *News* editors, Darwin P. Kingsley and Edwin Price, were ashamed of the patrons and had delayed writing about them, as the majority were friends of the newspaper. One can sense the deep sighs between the printed words and that the editors regretted the need for such stringent sentiments.

For over a year, the *News* had been educating its weatherworn readers on how a civilized population functions. Humor and delicate language gently reformed, but change came slowly. The Western Slope's sensibilities were still in the tanning process.

The problem of the opium dens brought out the town's rough side. The article applauded efforts to rid the town of such unsavory establishments but advocated a civilized way. It was talking about one man in particular who actively favored violence over reason. Earlier in the week, "Buck" Gilliland had roused citizens to near mob lunacy. The editors were equally perturbed by the town's mayor, A.A. Miller, who was quietly cheering him on.

They beseeched Miller to get control of the situation and to protect all the citizens of Grand Junction. They cited Yep Mow, the first Chinese man in town and a Christianized business owner, who had applied for citizenship. He had a right to protection, they claimed, as did all the Chinese.

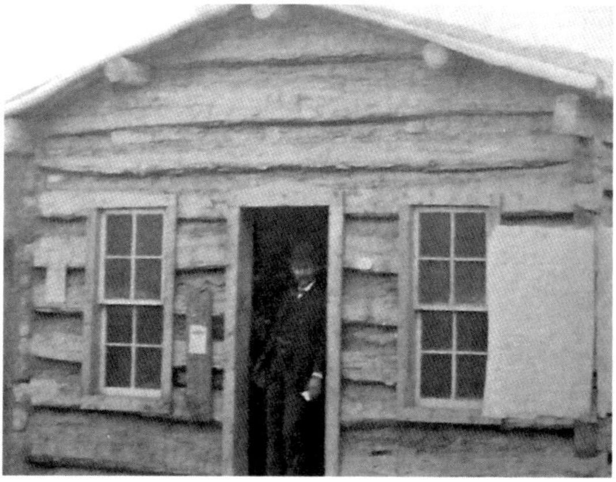

Edwin Price and his brother brought their newspaper printer and equipment from Denver via buckboard wagon. When Edwin first saw the greasewood landscape of the Western Slope, he almost turned around. His adventurous spirit urged him on, and he established the *Grand Junction News* in a log cabin in October 1882. Darwin P. Kingsley soon joined him, and with their wit and wisdom, they proceeded to sculpt and polish the pioneer town. *Courtesy of Loyd Files Research Library.*

Mayor Miller did little to staunch the flow of hatred. His idea of controlling the situation was joining the mob for a drink and asking them to settle down for now. He promised that in a few days he'd "give them liberty to carry out their scheme."

Gilliland was arrested on Friday night after shooting at his boss, Thomas Keehn, over a misunderstanding. When he was able to post bail, he found his compatriots and exhorted them to move forward with the ousting. Gilliland's bondsman heard about the rumor and demanded he be re-arrested. He was, after the city marshal found the man hiding—in Mayor Miller's office.

Emotions were high that night, and the mob, sans Gilliland, decided to forgo the mayor's offer. They assembled to swarm down Colorado Avenue, where the Chinese population lived. Sheriff Martin Florida ordered Captain T.B. Crawford, of Company F, to muster his men. They stood guard all weekend. From Friday night, August 17, through Monday night, August 20, citizens slept with guns under their pillows.

Due to strong feelings against the wayward mayor, Miller changed camps on Monday and came out against the marauders, but he emphasized it was not because it was illegal, just that it was in the wrong hands.

Reason finally prevailed. The Chinese stayed, and the opium dens—none of which, it turned out, was operated by the Chinese citizens—departed.

# Have Toy Gun Will Travel

The editors of the *Grand Junction News* were extremely loquacious on many subjects and used the printed word to affect politics, booster the town and, as we've seen, act as judges on unsavory elements in town. They also had their fingers in any intriguing pot that presented itself. When a genuine Indian scare made Grand Junction "feel for their scalps," *News* editor D.P. Kingsley took up arms, as well as the printed word, to save his beloved city.

It was the summer of 1883, and heat sweltered the valley citizens. The mercury climbed to "panic" on Wednesday, June 13, when two Fruita men rode hard into town. Mopping their brows with shaky hands, they reported that they'd just encountered some Ute who'd been on the warpath for two horse thieves.

Eight braves and several squaws (or young braves, the man couldn't tell which) had forced their way into their home and insisted on being fed. While eating, they'd relayed the shooting of "Jack and Charley" for stealing some horses and insisted that the occurrence "be written down for the 'Big

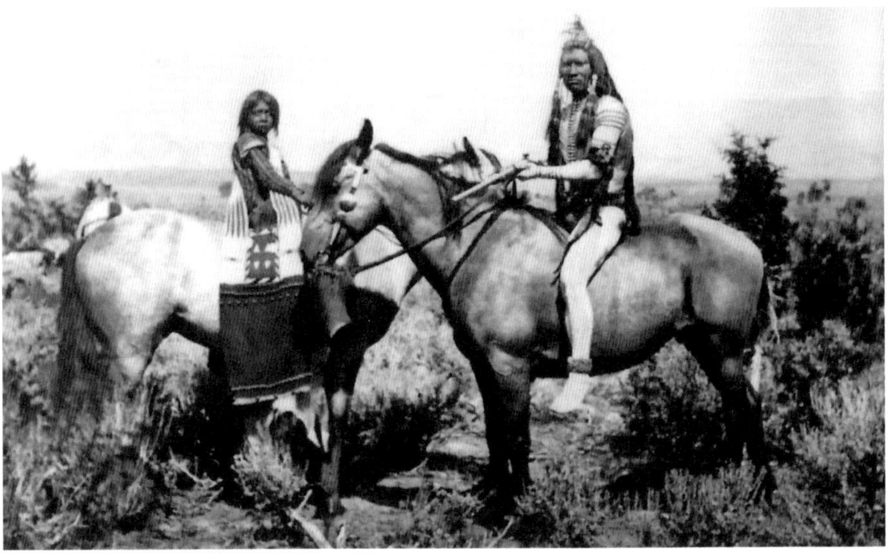

Ute Indians had been driven from their home in the valley in September 1881 but often left their Utah reservation and visited the Western Slope. It was not usually a happy occasion for the new citizens of the valley. Newspapers mentioned them riling up ranchers when they hunted areas dry, leaving little for others. Ute chased down horse thieves through the valley and sometimes demanded food from quaking mothers and children. Fear of Indians was intense, and even a whiff of an attack set everyone on their toes. *Courtesy of National Archives and Records Administration (NARA), ID 517733.*

Captain' at Grand Junction." They also asked about how many troops were in the valley and were informed that there were about five hundred. It was an exaggeration, but upon learning that, the Ute hopped on their horses and sped toward the Utah trail.

Their story seemed a bit crazy, so the *News* editors rallied the townsfolk to see who would go with Kingsley to check out the story. Not much enthusiasm was shown, probably because everyone wanted to keep their scalps. One "valiant" Company F soldier offered fifteen dollars to any substitute. Finally, about 9:00 p.m., seasoned lawman L.R. Ketchum and Messrs Thatcher and Sechrest rode off into the sunset. G.S. Harrington, a local businessman, and *News* editor Kingsley joined forces and set off after them.

Kingsley described the scene: "We were armed to the teeth; Harrington had on a leather girdle that reached from his hips up under his arms, struckfull [*sic*] of ferocious looking cartridges, while to his right side was hitched a bran [*sic*] new double-action six-shooter—to say nothing of a huge white hat which made him look quite terrible." Kingsley went armed with a toy pistol and a "dirty handkerchief" in his hip pocket.

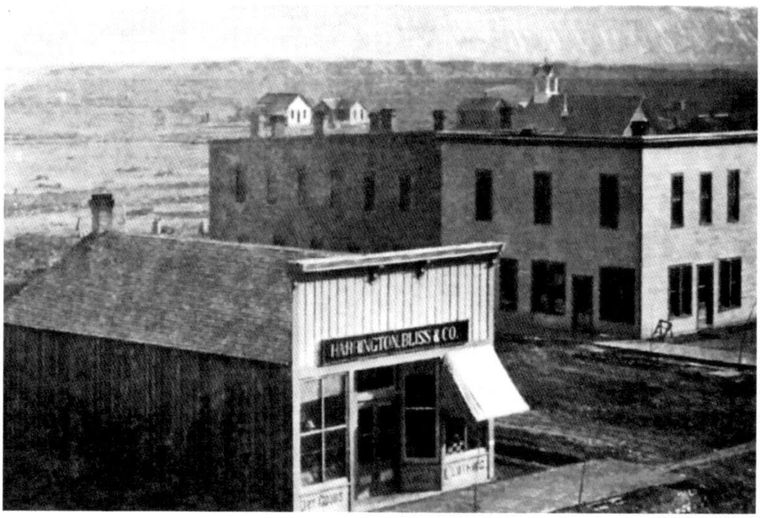

Harrington and Bliss partnered a successful mercantile business. After Harrington left town, Bliss continued the business for many decades. This is the northwest corner of Main Street and Fifth. After Bliss moved his business down the street, this building became the first home of the First National Bank. It was torn down in 1890 to build a beautiful Victorian home, but construction materials deteriorated. A new yellow brick went up in 1910, and an addition was added in 1920. *Courtesy of Loyd Files Research Library.*

They set out west hoping to discover the bodies somewhere along the way. After about a half mile of riding, they happened upon a young boy half sleeping on a load of wood. Harrington asked him if he knew anything about the "Indian murders" down valley, and the "boy's eyes opened and came out of his head like a jack in a box." He knew nothing but wanted to know everything.

Undeterred by ignorance, the men continued their trek and about six miles west came to a ranch, where a woman and a boy stood in the doorway. The pertinent question was asked, and the woman emphatically agreed that it was all true. She pointed to two cabins about a mile away and said the men who had been shot were lying there.

Away they went, "and found at the cabin(s) not even the suspicion of a drop of blood, nor a trace of a foot." Disappointed, they urged their steeds to speed up to reach Ketchum and company. As they approached a knoll, they saw a group of men on the other side.

Skittish, Harrington cried, "Gee whiz, it's them Utes." Kingsley responded by drawing his toy gun, prepared to die with all his wounds "in front." It turned out it was only their fellow countrymen. Chagrined, the two men cantered up to them.

Ketchum, who knew a lot about Indians, was deciphering the ground. Some kind of fracas had happened here, that's for sure. All signs showed that the horse thieves had gathered at the cabin and the Ute had sprung upon them, rounding up the ponies. Blood and bodies, however, were nowhere to be seen. Tracks showed moccasins heading one way and shoed horses heading toward Grand Junction.

It was obvious to the posse that the Ute had exaggerated a little themselves. The horse thieves had been here, and it looked like they'd left with their plunder. The posse decided they weren't going to be made fools of, and when they arrived back home, Ketchum put out a telegram to all the outlying railroad stations to be on the lookout for Jack and Charley. Kingsley did his part, and every last sordid detail was printed in the *News*.

George Root, editor of the *White Pine Cone*, in Gunnison County, wrote his tongue-in-cheek, albeit skewed, take on the scare. It was lovingly reprinted in the *Grand Junction News* on June 30, 1883:

> *They have had an Indian scare at Grand Junction. A party of horse thieves run off a few head of ponies belonging to the Utes, taking them to the Grand Valley. The tribe of Chipeta resented this appropriation of their property, followed the thieves, and recovered their stock. But the appearance*

> *of the* [Ute] *created the wildest excitement in Grand Junction. The men hid in outhouses and sand pits, women fainted and the authorities were paralyzed with terror. It is said that the sheriff, Florida, was discovered two days afterward, wedged so tightly in the chimney of an unoccupied building that he could not get out. When they dragged him out, he gasped, "please Mr. Indian, don't scalp me, I'm a Mormon!" When the excitement was at its height, Lt. D.P. Kingsley, the handsome and talented editor of* The Grand Junction News, *appeared in the midst of the terrified throng and offered to lead a posse to exterminate the* [Ute]. *After much persuasion he succeeded in getting one man to accompany him, and arming themselves to the shirt collar, the intrepid leader rode off at the head of his little band in search of the enemy. But the* [Ute] *had started for Utah, and although the Lt. followed them many weary miles, he failed to even get a glimpse of them. Thus was blood war averted.*

Kingsley responded: "That UTE business put a feather in our hat at least."

Darwin Pearl Kingsley rode his horse up the political and corporate ladder, eventually becoming the president of New York Life and a national speaker. He's known for the motto: "You have powers you never dreamed of. You can do things you never thought you could do. There are no limitations in what you can do except the limitations of your own mind." It could be said that he learned this firsthand on the wild Western Slope.

## Roan Creek Eek!

Indian scares kept Colorado pioneers on the alert. In August and September 1887, the warlike White River Ute were stirring up the settlers again in northwestern Colorado near Meeker. Since the Meeker Massacre of 1879, any whisper of a warpath transformed farmers and townsfolk into instant soldiers. On September 3, 1887, word got to the folks on Roan Creek, near De Beque, that some Ute, possibly from White River, had been seen camping near the river. Ears perked up immediately, and guns were quickly leaned against windows and doors.

The three boys who encountered them gave chase, according to their tale, but were outdistanced. A "small scare was established," wrote the *News*. Dr. W.A.E. De Beque took off on his "bronco" with a Winchester to give him courage. Several other men stuffed their fear under their ten-gallon hats and joined him. They "galloped boldly off to find the foes."

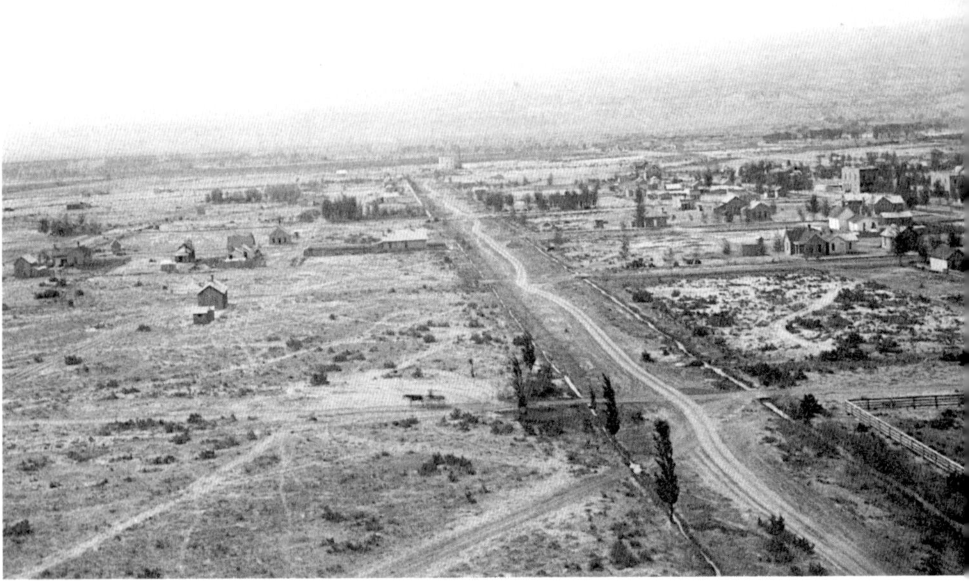

Meanwhile, the wives and mothers worked on escape plans and "ignored their home duties."

Searching Dr. De Beque's homestead, Ravensbeque, first, they pressed on to scour land between Roan Creek and the Grand River. Not one Indian was discovered. The *News* was blunt in its belief that the boys had generated one whopping lie. It assured its readers, "At last accounts, all was quiet along the turbid waters of the Roan."

## YOU DON'T MESS AROUND WITH HIM

Indian scares aside, Western Slope citizens dealt with frontier challenges deftly. The occasional lynch mob was circumvented, cattle rustlers and horse thieves were generally corralled and most murderers were handled in the appropriate and legal way. Every once in a while, a situation came up where the moral lines were a bit wavy, and the public wrestled with their admiration of a job well done and a desire to be a sophisticated town.

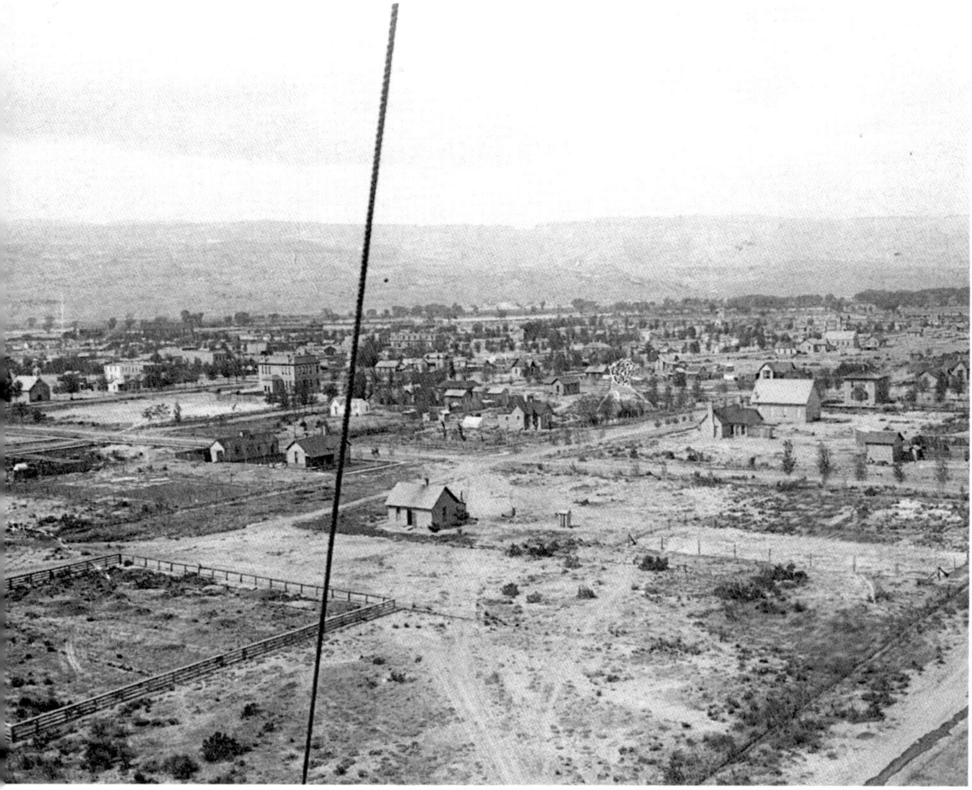

This 1889 aerial photo, possibly taken from a hot air balloon or the top of the old water standpipe at Seventh and Chipeta, shows a town spreading its boundaries in every direction. The wagon road heading due south, on the left side of the picture, is Seventh Street, and the one heading due west is the future Grand Avenue. The first town plat outlined the town from North Avenue to South Avenue and from First Street to Twelfth Street. *Courtesy of Loyd Files Research Library.*

One such occasion was when Alexander Struthers, master mechanic for the Denver & Rio Grande Railroad, shot a man dead. A few weeks after 1895 had been birthed, Struthers was walking home from the rail yards with his hands in his pockets. It was just after 9:00 p.m., and it was cold. He lived on South Fifth Street, near the bridge, a little ways from the railroad yards where he worked.

He had just turned onto the wide avenue of South Fifth when he saw ahead of him two men walking rapidly toward him. Just before they reached him, Struthers heard whispering, and then the cock of two guns sounded clearly in the night air.

"Hold up your hands, you ____ _____ _____ _____, or I'll fill you full of lead!" One of the men shouted the warning while his partner sidled up to the mechanic's left. A former lawman in another state, Struthers knew how to handle himself. As he pulled his hands from his pockets, he brought out his six shooter and, within a second, had shot the chatty one in the left breast.

The wounded man got off a shot, too, and a ball ripped through Struthers's right pants pocket. Stumbling away from Struthers, he managed to run several feet toward the river before he collapsed, dying. The other man scurried toward town but turned back several times to shoot at Struthers, who emptied his gun in both directions. The man kept running and disappeared into the shadows. Struthers got the idea he'd been hit.

Struthers rushed home to reload his gun and start the hunt for the escapee. When he arrived back on scene, his neighbor, Mike Kelleher, stood over the body, and a crowd had gathered. Among them were a *News* reporter and the coroner, who knew that flying bullets usually meant a body or two.

The dead man, who would later prove to be Denverite William DeFoe, had perished from a bullet to the heart. It was presumed that the other man was injured and would show up somewhere needing help. DeFoe was identified by Ed Shick, a man who had come to Grand Junction with DeFoe in December and roomed with him. Shick was checked to see if he was the escaped suspect, but not being injured, he was dismissed.

When Struthers got home that night, five bullets had knocked holes in his clothing but miraculously missed all body parts. A coroner's jury found that Alexander Struthers was innocent of murder and had justifiably killed DeFoe. The *News* had its illustrator draw pictures of the drama and printed them alongside a detailed account of the evening's exciting events.

Relatives of the dead man telegraphed for the remains to be shipped to Denver, which they were. The other robber never did show up.

## Motorcycle Madness

Felix Carson was another town citizen who didn't take crime lying down. He'd been lying down, however, at 4:00 a.m. on Saturday, September 28, 1912, when police informed him that his motorcycle shop had been broken into. He rushed down to the corner of Seventh and Main, where he found one of his best cycles stolen. The thief had broken the north side window to open the door, glommed onto a seven-horsepower Excelsior cycle, worth $350, and, evidently having time on his hands, perused the array of cycles waiting for repair, looking for a better seat. He exchanged the standard one on the Excelsior for the better one belonging to E. Frank Winford's machine. He then filled the tank with gasoline and left.

Felix suspected a man he knew. He rousted A.C. Schwenker out of bed, and the two of them hastened off on motorcycles. They headed toward Delta. On Saturday evening, they called with news of farmers seeing a man hightailing down the outlying roads on a motorcycle. He fit the description of the suspect. One farmer reported him taking a spill five miles north of Delta, but that hadn't deterred the thief. He'd picked himself up and, at a high rate of speed, pursued his escape.

Determined to catch the man, Carson and Schwenker made "a complete tour" of the farming section looking for clues. The two men returned dejected to Grand Junction on Sunday. Carson's ride to Delta was reported as "very spectacular." Mr. Schwenker said, "I could not stay with Carson at all. He was mad clear through and rode like a demon."

He had the sympathy of the town for his keen loss, but Carson was hopeful the authorities would find his cycle.

The matter did not end there. On October 2, the *Grand Junction Daily Sentinel* reported "one of the worst examples of bone-headedness ever recorded." The authorities at Olathe had finally caught the gent who'd stolen the machine. The thief gave his name as Joe Perry. He was twenty-three years old, five foot six or seven and wore a cowboy hat and black coat over his blue overalls. Perry had filed off the motorcycle's number and stripped it of "extra equipment," but it was Carson's machine, all right.

Sheriff Charles Schrader was informed of the arrest and that Perry would be brought to Montrose for pickup. The authorities had a dilemma, though—how to get the motorcycle *and* the thief to Montrose. Their scheme was to allow Perry to mount the machine and order him to ride slowly while they followed in the car. Perry followed orders "meekly" until he got the machine started, and before the authorities had settled in their seats, Perry "opened the throttle" and popped "out of sight at about 60 miles an hour."

Felix Carson didn't mince words about the whole escapade. Sheriff Schrader just shook his head and sent out "hundreds of post cards" with descriptions of the criminal and the vehicle. He set a reward of fifty dollars for the capture of both.

Several weeks later, the motorcycle was found in Montrose, in pretty good shape for its wild adventure, and returned to Carson. Joe Perry, apparently not partial to any particular style of travel, was in jail for stealing a horse.

Perhaps it was the robbery, but Carson moved to a larger, more secure location at 639 Main Street shortly afterward. He soon became the sole

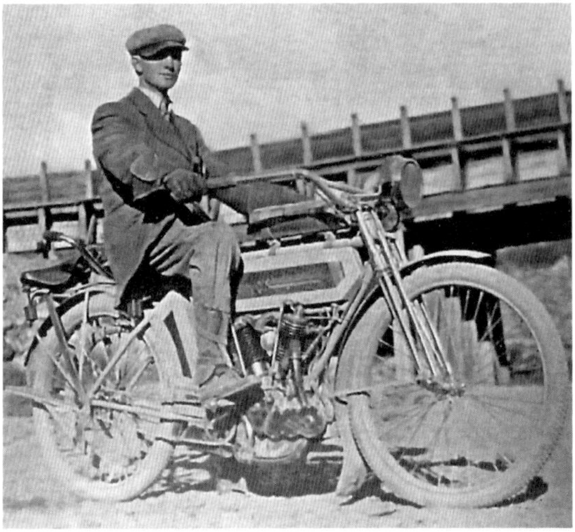

Felix Carson was the first Harley Davidson dealer in the valley. His second shop was at 629–31 Main Street. He ran it until he died in 1919 from the Spanish influenza. He left behind a widow and two boys. His brother, Porter, took up the business when he returned from World War I, moving the shop to 329 Main. Felix and Porter were the biggest early promoters of motorcycles and bicycles, setting up races and donating heavily to local events. *Courtesy of Matt Carson.*

agent for Harley-Davidson motorcycles, and business thrived. Felix Carson was to enjoy his success only another seven years. He died in 1919, at the age of thirty-one.

## The Lady and the Twisted Tale

A stylishly dressed young woman stepped off Rio Grande No. 3 car in April 1907. This step introduced a most bizarre tale. A week before, a young man by the name of Howard Smith had been shot and killed in Clifton, a few miles east of Grand Junction. His robbing the safe of a Grand Junction livery owned by Barton & Terrill started the curious journey. He'd run off after absconding with almost $100 in coin and cash.

Clifton businessmen were suspicious of the man, who came into their stores buying new attire to replace worn-out clothes. Hearing a safe had been robbed in Grand Junction, one man, H.E. Munson, called the sheriff and was deputized to take young Smith into custody until the authorities arrived. All seemed well until Smith decided to bolt. Munson gave chase after firing several bullets into the ground. Smith kept going, so Munson thought to injure him in order to stop him. Aiming for his leg, he fired, but just at that moment, Smith stepped into a small ditch, lowering his body about twenty inches. The bullet meant for a leg found its mark in his heart.

Several days later, after the news reached Denver, a young woman called undertaker E.A. Krohn's parlors, where the body, slated for a pauper's grave, lay. She asked Mr. Krohn to describe the man, and she decided it was her long-lost brother. Via train, she arrived in Grand Junction and verified the body as her brother. She made arrangements for it to be sent to his old home in Clarksburg, West Virginia.

A few days later, Krohn received unsettling news. Lo and behold, the body wasn't that of Howard Scott Smith, who, in reality, was six feet tall, forty years old and very much alive. The young man Krohn had shipped was five feet five inches and in his early twenties. Even stranger, after denying this man was the real Howard Smith, the West Virginians decided to bury the body anyway in their own family cemetery. Southern hospitality?

Miss Rose Lee Smith, the mysterious lady from Denver, finally wrote a letter to the newspaper and explained herself. After making the trip to town, she had doubts this man was her brother but had recently met a man named Howard Scott Smith, of West Virginia. She decided to give the young man this name and arrange for him to be sent to that state so at least he'd have a decent burial.

After learning that "young" Smith wasn't the elder Smith, a deeper investigation turned up army deserter Harry Swiger of Williamsburg, West Virginia. In the same company as Rose's brother, when Harry deserted, he assumed Rose's brother's name in order to elude the authorities. Miss Smith took full responsibility for the crazy events.

## *Chapter 3*

# The Art of Flight

*Our jail is not able to keep a prisoner in or any party out.*
—Grand Junction News, *August 1885*

The first Grand Junction jail was a hewn-log box located a little east of Third Street between Main and Colorado. It was dubbed the calaboose and was built by private scrip in early 1882. The *Grand Junction News* didn't set out its shingle until October of that year, so the city's early recorded history, especially its crime, is limited. Western Slope lawmen didn't always get their prisoner, but a valiant effort was generally applied.

On November 4, 1882, the *News* remarked on the first-ever city jailbreak. A man, name unknown, had stolen a gun from Mr. Fitzpatrick, who manned the Grand (Colorado) River ferry. He was found, arrested and incarcerated in the small edifice. It was customary for the jailer to leave prisoners unchained during the day and then, after feeding them dinner, to secure them for the night. That winter evening, the jailer did just that and then went home to his own supper and slumber.

The crook had at least one ally, albeit one with a few cards short of a full deck. After the jailer left, the friend approached the jail under the cover of darkness and set the heavy wooden door on fire. His jail buddy nearly died of smoke inhalation before help arrived. By that time, a sizeable opening had been forged with the flames. The fire was quickly extinguished. With no pity dispatched in his direction, the prisoner was chained to the floor to await morning. Frigid air blanketed him, but not for long. Somehow, the man broke free of his chains and escaped out the gap in the door. Perhaps that was the plan all along, and he was never seen again. This was the beginning of a long queue of jailbreaks in Mesa County.

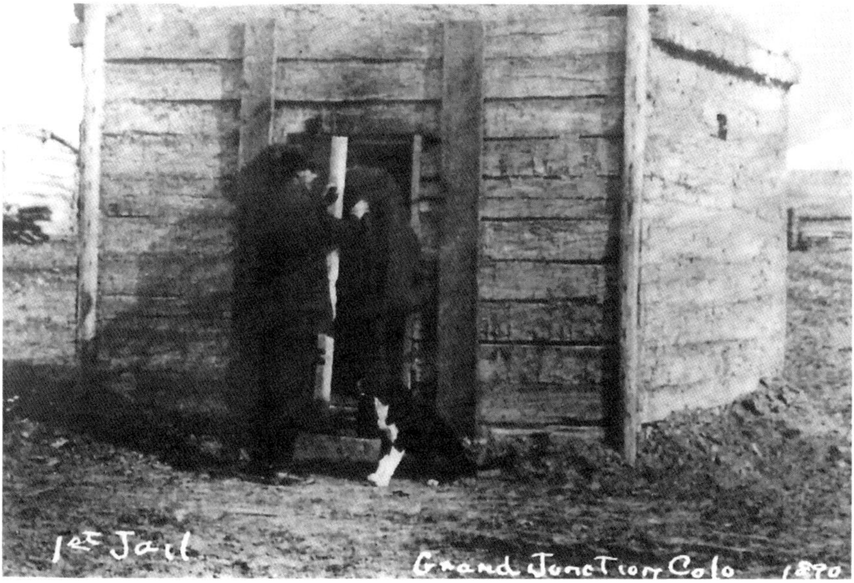


The first jail was built by scrip in early 1882. Today, it would be located on the alley between Main and Colorado Avenue, slightly east of Third Street. After the jail moved to the new building on Fifth and Colorado, the old log cabin was used for various things, lastly an unsightly landscape for tattered posters. Locals pushed to save the historic building, and it was moved to Lincoln Park. No one knows what happened to it from then on. *Courtesy of Loyd Files Research Library.*

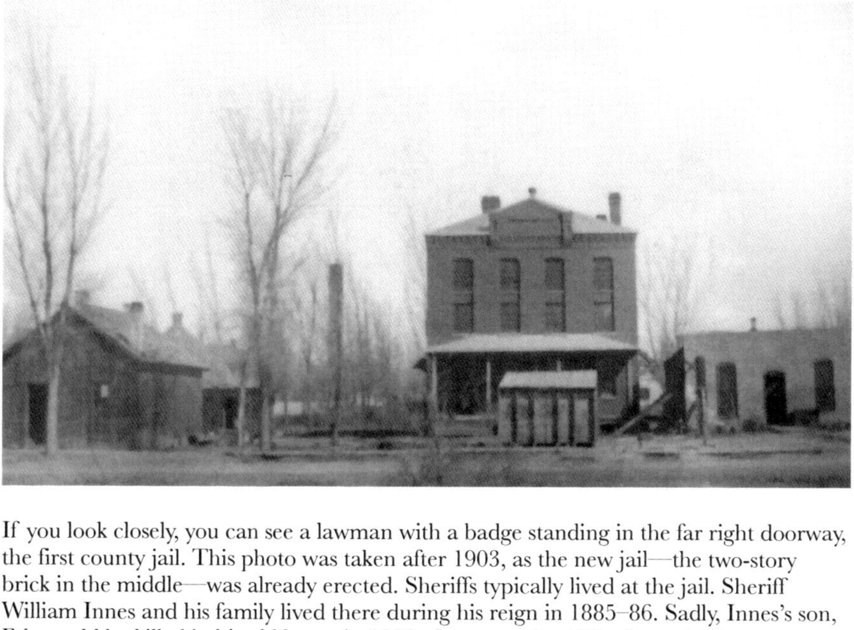

If you look closely, you can see a lawman with a badge standing in the far right doorway, the first county jail. This photo was taken after 1903, as the new jail—the two-story brick in the middle—was already erected. Sheriffs typically lived at the jail. Sheriff William Innes and his family lived there during his reign in 1885–86. Sadly, Innes's son, Ed, would be killed in his old home in 1906. *Courtesy of Loyd Files Research Library.*

By September 1884, a new city jail was under construction, a brick one this time, embedded in cement. It was paid for by city scrip and located on the southwest corner of Colorado Avenue and Fifth Street. In a few years, this corner would also house the newly formed fire department.

The county jail builders weren't as experienced as the city's were. The first county jail was built on White Avenue, midway between Seventh and Eighth Streets, on the north side. It was a wood frame building, and it might as well have had a swinging door. Escape after escape exasperated the population, and eventually citizens just rolled their eyes and said, "What's new?" when the paper reported another one.

## Harry Hahn on Halloween

Attempted escapes were plenty, and neither jail seemed a challenge for Harry Hahn on Halloween Eve 1885. He'd been pronounced insane and was scheduled for transportation to Pueblo soon. Even in his fragile mental state, he knew he didn't want to go to an asylum. He broke out of the city jail on Friday and was later found hiding in the *News* office. Hoping the county jail could hold the cagey fellow, he was incarcerated there. On Saturday morning, he again tried to escape. The lawmen were waiting for him this time, and at his capture, he roused the whole upper section of town with his loud cries.

## Burning the Midnight Foil

Another escape plan was stopped by Deputy Sheriff Charley Knowles, who was no idiot. When he noticed that magazines and then a peach carton weren't returned by some prisoners, he kept an eye on the bunch. One of the men was Robert Kennedy, who'd coldheartedly left a man he'd beaten and robbed lying on the railroad tracks for the oncoming train to rend asunder. Searching his cell and clothes, Knowles found a case knife and interviewed prisoners. He learned that at night Kennedy, who was a machinist, had been burning the magazines near the bars to temper the steel so he could cut through them. The rest of the prisoners had watched the process with keen interest, visions of escape dancing in the flames. Their hopes went up in smoke now that the plan was blown out. All prisoners remained present and accounted for, and Knowles's suspicious mind thwarted one of the biggest jailbreak schemes in the county's history.

## A Hole in One

The funniest attempt at escape made the front page of the *Sentinel* on June 29, 1906. At the time, the city jail was connected to the back of the fire station at the southwest corner of Colorado Avenue and Fifth Street.

W.H. Sanders had been "in an exaggerated state of intoxification" near the Presbyterian church. He'd been hauled off to jail and, that evening, came out of his stupor enough to notice the nice-sized hole in the back brick wall. Some earlier, and unsuccessful, escape artist had left a great big temptation for Sanders, who felt he needed another drink.

A crowbar was nary to be found, so the prisoner used part of the stove to chip away at the opening. The firehouse flanked the jail to the north. Fire Chief Perry Rogers and his men heard Sanders's commotion right away but decided they'd wait outside the jail yard fence and re-arrest the man once he'd escaped.

Sanders was a small man and soon scrambled through the expanded hole to highly anticipated freedom. Following his example was a fellow inmate

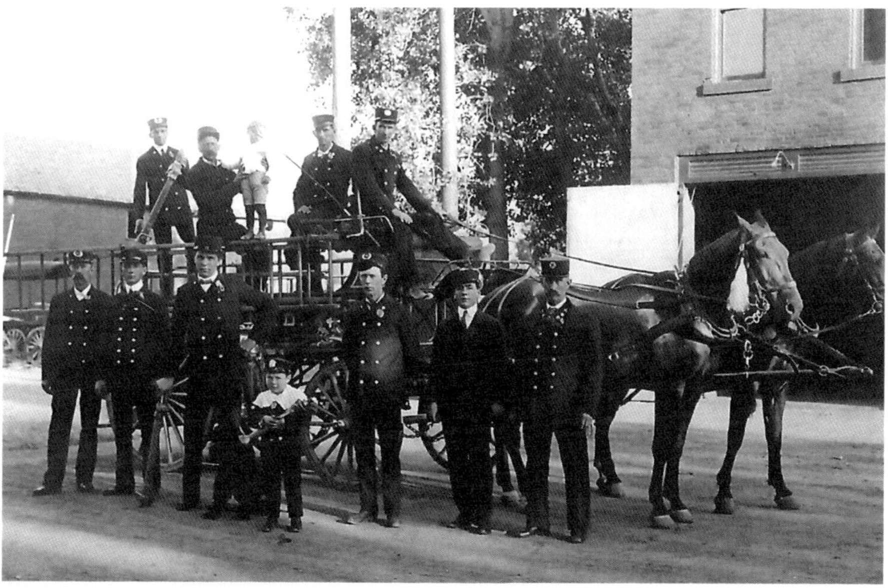

Before an official fire department was formed, Grand Junction had two volunteer teams. Around 1890, they moved into the first floor of city hall at Colorado and Fifth. The jail was at the back, on the alley. This building held court on that corner until the 1970s, when, as an Army Surplus store, arson burned it to the ground. Nothing has been built on it since. *Courtesy of Loyd Files Research Library.*

who wasn't so small—he got stuck. Noticing his predicament, Sanders attacked the wall around his companion's derriere, and if it weren't for a snicker in the general direction of the fence, he might have made it out, too.

Turning around slowly, Sanders saw Chief Rogers's gun pointed at him, and he threw his hands as high as he could, even standing on his toes to show how willing he was to give up. The man in the hole had to be helped back in. The two erstwhile prisoners were confined "closely" after that. The hole was filled in immediately.

## YULETIDE LAM

The Mesa County jail's first official escapee may have been helped along by the first sheriff, Martin Florida. Florida had quite a life story. According to his obituary, he was a Canadian who'd been injured and then captured for a time by the Spanish while on a "filibustering" expedition in Cuba. His careers spanned mining, railroad construction and even teaching at the Indian school in Grand Junction. In Gunnison County, he'd been justice of the peace before migrating to the Western Slope, where he became the new county's first sheriff. He sported a legendary reputation as having captured Brigham Young at the Mountain Meadow Massacre in Utah in 1857.

It was the day before Christmas Eve 1884 when the escape happened. Henry Herrick had shot and killed his wife at their Whitewater ranch and had then been arrested. This saga began a few months prior, after Henry took up with another woman and raised the ire of his wife. Mrs. Herrick had shot and killed the pregnant mistress as she sat next to Mr. Herrick on a wagon. She was jailed and, while behind bars, secured a divorce from her husband.

Two days before Christmas, Sheriff Florida chaperoned her, along with a young man, to the Whitewater ranch to round up her portion of the family riches, mainly cattle. Knowing Mr. Herrick wouldn't be happy with this errand, Florida told Mrs. Herrick to stay low while he gathered the cattle. He was searching nearby when he heard a shot ring out.

According to the young man, who'd stayed with the lady, Herrick had approached them and assaulted Mrs. Harrick with "all manner of vile language" and ordered her to leave. She started to leave, "and when her back was turned, Herrick fired."

The young man ran to her, and she said, "He has killed me at last." The buckshot shattered her left arm and back. By this time, Florida had run back to his charge and found her dead. Angry more at himself than anything, he found Herrick, who was about to jump on a horse and skedaddle, and arrested him.

Florida was shocked that the man would shoot Mrs. Herrick, especially in the back, and said so. "Is she dead?" Herrick asked. Then he told Florida it was an accident.

The *News* editors thought it was lucky Florida got to him before the area citizens had. They felt he would have been "riddled with bullets" if caught by them.

Mr. Herrick now stood where his ex-wife had been just hours before—behind bars. After escorting Herrick to his cell, the sheriff left, taking the prisoner's clothing with him for some unknown reason. He also left the door unlocked. When Florida returned later, he putzed around in the office and then left without performing his usual routine of securing the prisoner. He didn't even check on him. The next morning, Florida stuck his head in the cell room and discovered it was empty. It being Christmas Eve, Florida wasn't inclined to start a search for Herrick just then. The whole affair made the *News* suspicious, and it encouraged Florida to assuage the questions by bringing Herrick back.

Florida finally took a hint and embarked on a westward train. He was gone four days, informing the authorities in towns around southern Utah to be on the lookout for Herrick. Sightings of him were few, but he was glimpsed briefly in Ogden before disappearing for good. The sheriff came home to leery glances.

He gave up law enforcement soon after and was much more successful at ranching.

## Bucklin Gets Beat

Harvey C. Bucklin's day on December 8, 1885, started out like any other. He was the genial jailer at the county jail. At the moment, the only inmates were J.H. Pierce and James Fogarty, horse thieves. The boys had just finished supper, and Bucklin was in the process of securing them for the night. While bending down, he was attacked from behind. One prisoner got ahold of Bucklin's body, and the other one slammed a bottle onto the left side of his head, knocking him unconscious. Blood began gushing from the deep cut, and the two men were afraid they'd gone and done it. After tying a cloth over his mouth and "ironing" Bucklin to the floor, they stole his money, six-shooter and a couple of blankets before escaping.

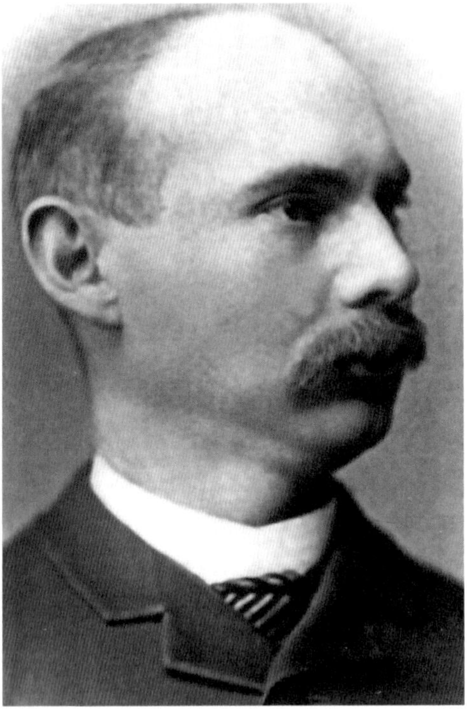

Just about any step in furthering the prominence of the Western Slope was attended by Harvey Bucklin. He was lauded by the *Sentinel* at the news of his death. He was a jack of all trades, and city directories attested to his many jobs over the years. His brother, A.N. Bucklin, was a noted lawyer. Both contributed to the growth of the valley. *Courtesy of Loyd Files Research Library.*

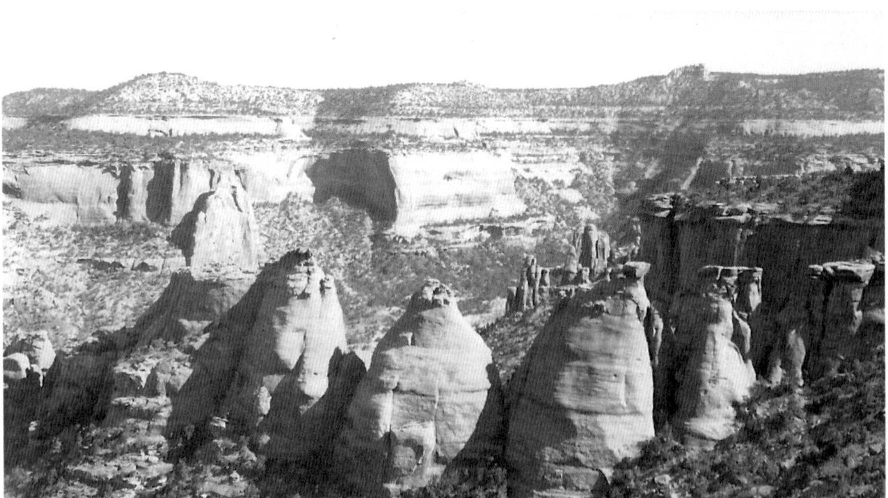

The Colorado National Monument just celebrated its 100th anniversary as a national park. John Otto can be credited almost entirely for this hauntingly beautiful place being designated so. He single-handedly crafted the trails that are enjoyed today. In the 1980s, the bicycle race Tour of the Moon annually careened around the hairpin roads. The movie *American Flyers*, centered on this race, shows some of the spectacular scenery. *Author's collection.*

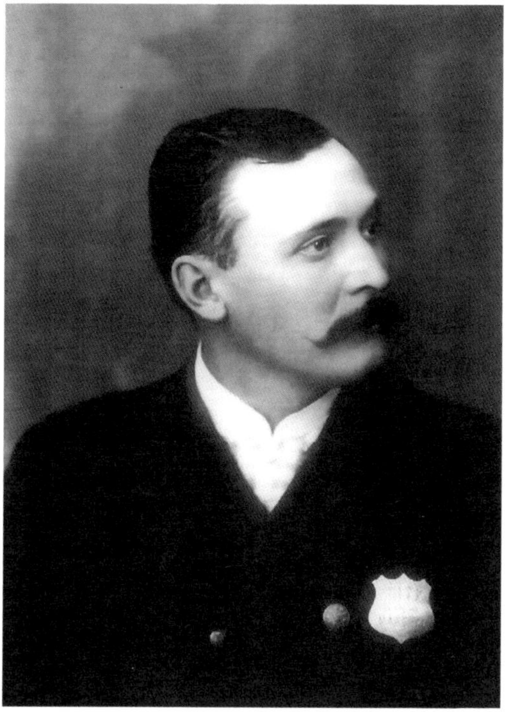

William Innes was elected twice into law enforcement. He was sheriff at one time and then marshal. This picture has been confused with that of his son, Edward Innes, who was never a marshal. Not only was Innes in law enforcement, but he also had a planing mill on Pinon Mesa for many years. His home was on the southwest corner of Chipeta and Eighth. *Courtesy of Loyd Files Research Library.*

It was a miracle that Harvey came to and was able to work his iron cuffs loose from the floor. Still chained, he hobbled to a nearby home for help. His wound was bound up, and twenty minutes later, a small posse was kicking up the snow.

Residents of Pinon Mesa, near today's Colorado National Monument, got suspicious of the two strangers who'd asked for food. After they left, Sheriff William Innes was notified, and the posse made its way west. They found the thieves huddled in a cold cabin, and they were returned to jail. After their trial, they served time in the penitentiary at Canon City.

Harvey's face was sliced from his temple down his cheek, and his doctor said he'd have bled out if he'd not been able to escape.

## Symphonic Reprieve

In 1886, Deputy Marshal Barney Kennedy conducted a drunk, Martin Pitts, to the city jail. The gent joined Marshal Hays, who was languishing in a cell that evening for some reason. Hays, in addition to being a lawman, was a member of the new brass band and had been allowed to bring his cornet with him.

Hoping to soothe his new cellmate, Hays blew a few notes from "Johnny, Go Get Your Gun." He was so enthralled by his own music that he failed to notice Pitts wasn't enjoying himself nearly as much as Hays was. As Hays played, Pitts got frustrated and whacked the brick wall nearest him, crumbling some of the mortar. Looking at it for a moment, he whacked a little more.

After starting a hole, Pitts decided to finish it, especially since Hays, possibly the deafest man around, seemed completely oblivious. When the hole was large enough, Pitts gratefully crawled into the corridor and found his way to the back door. He wrenched off the lock and ran across the yard, where he scaled the board fence to blessed peace and quiet. Pitts was soon recaptured, and when he appeared before the judge, he was fined seventeen dollars. The judge, knowing of Hays's dubious musical talents, did allow that Pitts's jailbreak was "justifiable."

## A Good Walk Spoiled

In 1903, a new county jail was constructed next to the old one on White Avenue. It didn't hold prisoners any better than the earlier one had. James Copeland, a forger who held the trustee position, was sent out one winter morning to get some coal for the stove. In spite of the temperature, the day was beautiful, and he decided that a nice walk in the fresh air would be a treat. He'd walked quite a distance when Deputy Sheriff Knowles realized he had never come back to the jail. He found him out by the Big Ditch and returned him home. Of course, he lost his trustee position.

## I Got You, Eddie!

Maybe if the county had done away with the trustee system, young jailer Ed Innes would have lived to be a grandfather. As it was, he was slain by George (aka John) McGarvey, who was in county jail for attempted rape. He'd been in long enough to become a trustee, and on the afternoon of September 24, 1906, he was cooking a meal in the county jail kitchen. McGarvey surreptitiously watched Innes, who intensely watched a card game progressing in a cell. He sat on the floor and didn't notice McGarvey

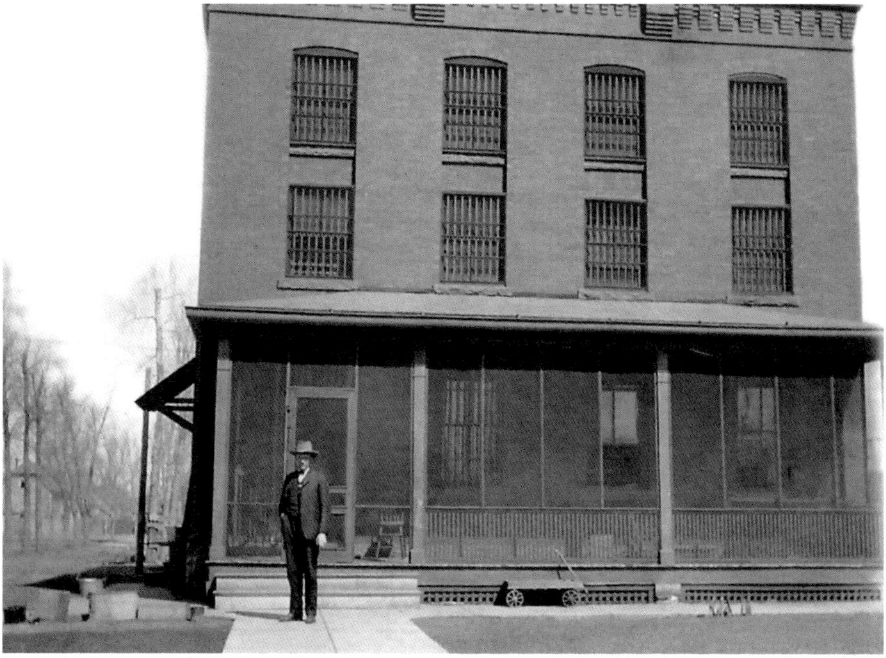

The north side of White Avenue, between Seventh and Eighth Streets, improved as neighborhoods spread outward. By the time this picture, with Sheriff Charles Schrader, was taken around 1908, Carnegie Library had been built catty-corner to the county jail. The old jail and outbuildings were long gone, and the grounds were beautified. Today, the parking lot for R-5 High School takes that spot. *Courtesy of Loyd Files Research Library.*

sneak up behind him. McGarvey smashed Innes's head with a two-by-four and knocked him unconscious. Blood flowed freely from a head wound. McGarvey used the jailer's own cuffs and fastened him to the cell bars. Gleefully, he jumped up and down and said, "I got you, Eddie!" He may not have realized he'd mortally wounded Innes as he ran out the door.

Some inmates reached through the bars to stop the blood, and others called out the window for help. Several neighbors passed by, ignoring the noise. Finally, the mailman decided to see what was going on and discovered Innes. He ran to find the sheriff, who contacted the lad's parents. Ed was too wounded to be transported anywhere, so they carried him upstairs to the sheriff's rooms.

A determined posse chased McGarvey's trail, but it was a De Beque rancher who sounded the alarm when McGarvey came to his back door and asked for food. He was a murderer by now. Innes had died around midnight without regaining consciousness.

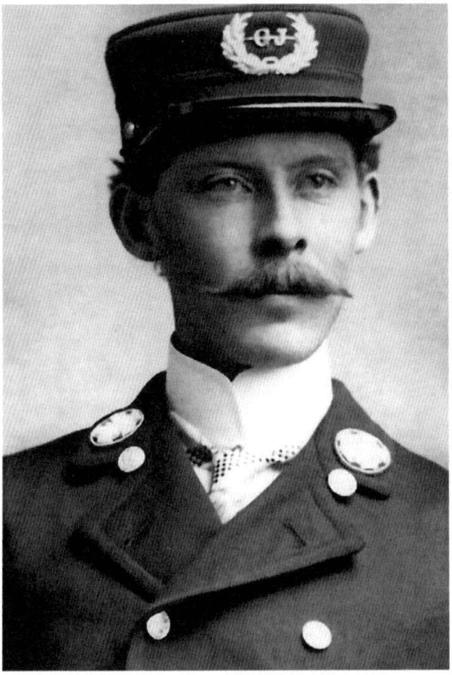

Edward Innes—Ed to his friends—was a young man when he was struck down at the jail. Well liked, he'd been associated with the fire department before becoming a jailer. He was the only lawman in Mesa County to die in the line of duty. Never married, he is buried alongside his parents at the Orchard Mesa Cemetery. *Courtesy of Loyd Files Research Library.*

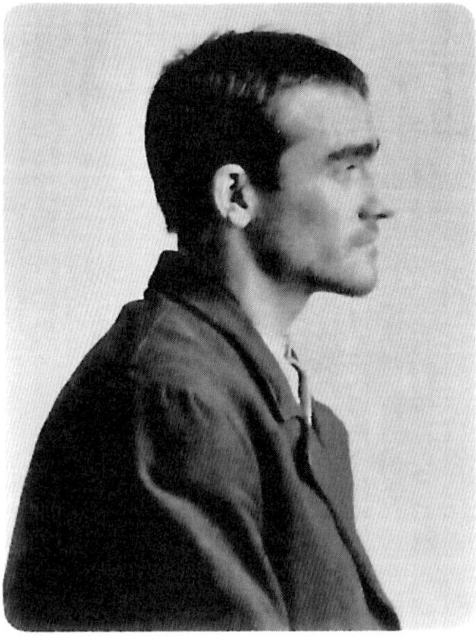

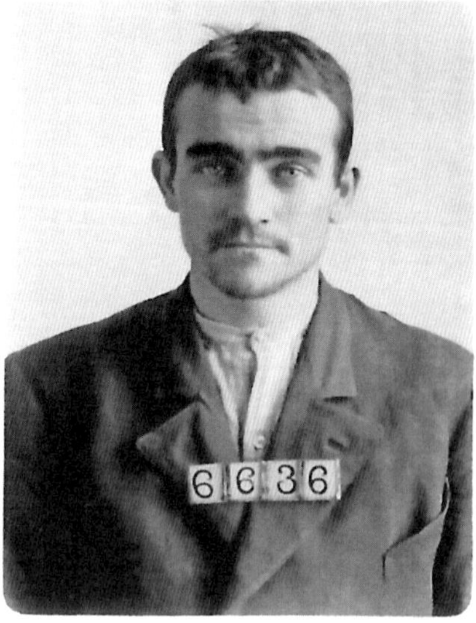


George McGarvey was dating a woman who worked at the St. Regis Hotel on Colorado at the time of his arrest. While visiting his girlfriend there, he accosted Gracie, the daughter of the owner, Harry Burnett. Accused of rape, he was placed in the county jail. The night he escaped, a posse searched for him until dark. They all sat around a fire near Watson Island on the Grand River, talking about what they'd do to McGarvey if they had the chance. Outside the warm glow of the fire, McGarvey listened and then slipped up the river toward De Beque. *Courtesy of Colorado State Archives.*

McGarvey's trial was swift, and he was pronounced guilty. He was sent to Canon City, where he carried a picture of his girlfriend under his prison garb. McGarvey was "launched" into eternity, via a self-activated hanging apparatus, the following January.

Ed Innes was the first law enforcer in Mesa County to perish in the line of duty. And though McGarvey's hanging rope was displayed in the city jail for many decades, the circumstances of Innes's tragic death were finally forgotten. A recent movement by some Grand Junction citizens finally got Innes the recognition he deserved. His name is now commemorated, along with other heroes of law enforcement, on the National Law Enforcement Officers' Memorial in Washington, D.C.

## Switched at Berth

In June 1931, a ring of four counterfeiters was arrested. The leader, W. Gayle Houk, was a handsome young man. His blond looks, natty dress and ready charm had served him well. He used several aliases; in Grand Junction, he was "Don Johnson." With this persona, he wore horn-rimmed glasses.

The foursome was arrested for counterfeiting one-dollar coins. Johnson and his co-conspirators had been hanging out at the county jail for a couple of months, being held for a U.S. grand jury. The county jail was now between Fifth and Sixth, on the south side of White Avenue. While awaiting their fate, Johnson hatched a plan to escape.

On August 2, 1931, Sheriff Charles Lumley was absent from the jail. Undersheriff Ralph Collinson stopped by to secure the prisoners for the night, leaving a friend in his vehicle at the curb. As was policy, he placed his .38-caliber revolver in the jail office while he performed this duty. When he opened the second-floor door, he was attacked by Johnson and Frank Randall, a local thief. They dragged Collinson into a cell and locked him in. Johnson ran down the stairs to get Collinson's gun. Just at that moment, coming through the door was Hugh Pinger, Collinson's friend, who was wondering what was taking so long. Johnson acted like he was a deputy and told Pinger that Collinson was in trouble upstairs and he should go help him. Pinger raced up the stairs, with Johnson right behind him carrying the undersheriff's gun. Pinger also wound up in a locked cell. Johnson offered any of the prisoners an escape, but only Randall and Charles Williams took him up on it.

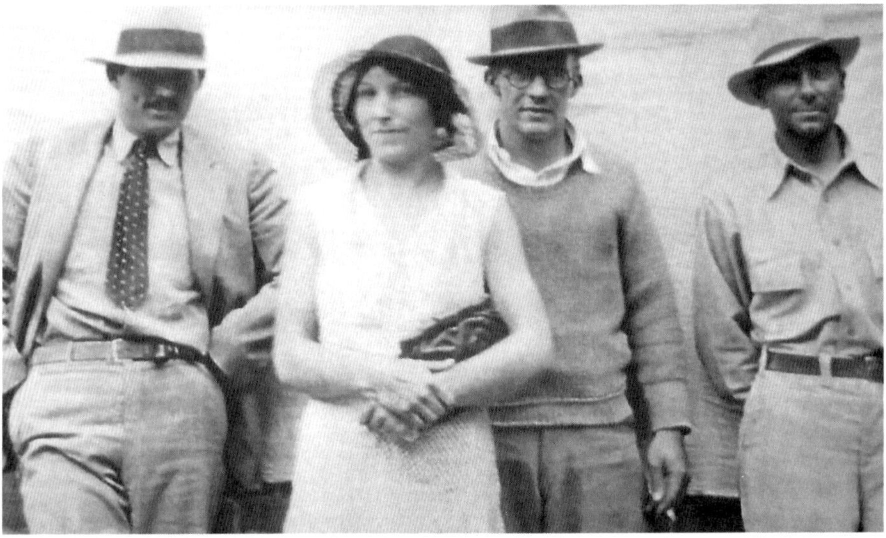

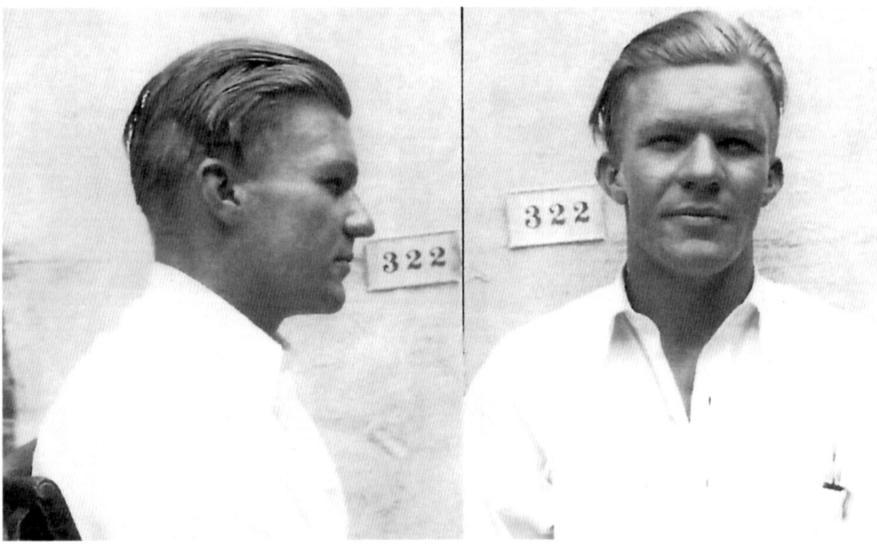


*This page*: Counterfeiting during the Depression seemed to be a solution for ready cash in a cash-strapped world. Members of Don Johnson's gang are probably the only counterfeiters ever caught on the Western Slope. After Houk escaped, it's unclear if he was ever captured again. *Courtesy of Teri Huff.*

Sheriff Lumley got word of what happened, and within a half hour, Williams was arrested on the north side of town. A day later, Randall was arrested in De Beque. Much to Lumley's disappointment, Johnson got clean away.

## A Jail Leak

The following Halloween, another escape occurred. The newspaper informed the public that Sheriff Lumley was begging the county to shore up the jail, as it was leaking prisoners. This time, two men made a "bold daylight break" when they sawed through an iron bar and beat another one awry so they could scrape through it. They jumped from the second-floor window. Sheriff Lumley found embedded footprints in the dirt underneath the window. The chase was on.

Word traveled over the wires, and Lumley heard that a woman and two men who fit the description of the escaped prisoners were seen in Cisco, Utah. The woman, driving a green Chevy with stolen plates, left Cisco and headed to Green River without the men. When she got there, she rented a hotel room. The Green River authorities were waiting when the two men finally showed up at her hotel room door later that day.

All three were arrested and sent back to Mesa County. It was then learned that the men had smuggled two bottles of acid into the jail right before their escape. They'd planned on blinding the guard with it if they'd not been able to escape through the bars.

## Lock and Key

The death of Marion Barton, city jail custodian, was "shrouded in mystery" when he was found sprawled on the floor of the jail corridor. Sheriff Charles H. Wallis discovered him at about three o'clock in the afternoon after seeing Sylvester Hill casually strolling down Fifth Street, away from the jail. Wallis was startled, as he had just dropped Hill off at the jail to await a hearing with a judge over whether he was "crazy" or not. He approached the prisoner carefully.

"What are you doing out, Hill?" asked the sheriff, to which the man lightly replied, "Oh, I am only taking a walk."

Wallis guided him back toward the jail, asking him how he got out in the first place. Hill told him he had a key and held it up. Wallis swiftly pocketed the key and then escorted him through the jail office door. It was then he saw a crumpled form on the floor. At that moment, he assumed it was "some drunk" Officer Allison had brought in for lockup.

On second glance, he realized it was Barton and rushed to his side. A phone call to the doctor was placed, but it took thirty minutes for one to arrive. The doctor tried to revive him, but "life was extinct," the *Sentinel* eulogized.

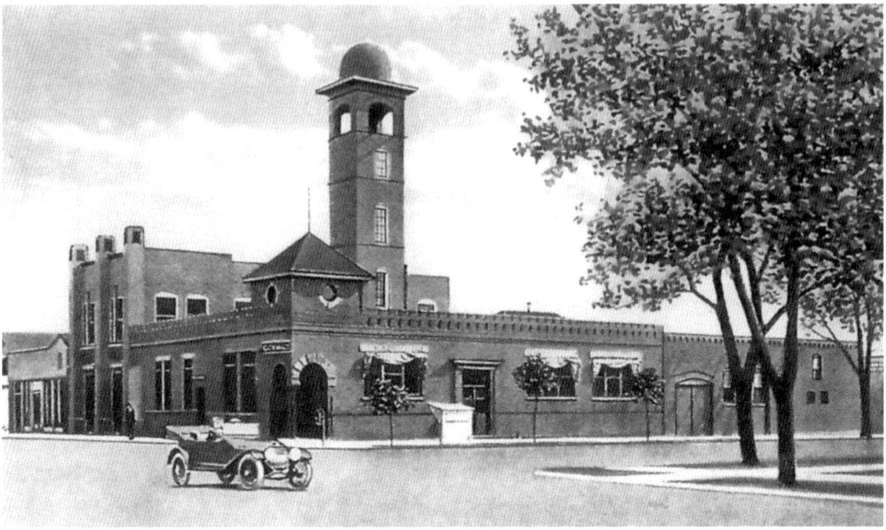

City hall moved one block east, to the southeast corner of Colorado and Sixth, before the fire department joined it with new training facilities. Even though this complex was better built, it still had its share of escapes. The buildings here were razed to put up a parking lot for the new State Office Building. *Author's collection.*

Dr. Henderson examined the body but could find no manner of death. Had Hill somehow killed the janitor in the process of leaving the jail? Lying next to the man was one of the cell's locks, but "the door leading into the corridor was locked by someone after Barton either died or was killed."

Hill was questioned intensely, but he was emphatic that Barton had given him the key. He said after Barton handed it to him, he laid down on the floor. Hill was afraid he'd be accused of hurting the man, so he walked out, locking the door behind him.

When news got out, "hundreds crowded to the city jail."

An autopsy was performed, concluding that the man, age thirty-four, had died from heart failure and a diseased liver.

## SCHOOL'S OUT FOREVER

Not every escape was from jail. Some considered school a jail, and when it came to keeping Indians behind classroom walls, it was certainly a challenge. The Grand Junction Indian School, later renamed the Teller Institute after Senator Henry Teller, was built in 1885. A couple of miles outside city limits, to the east, its purpose was to educate and house youth from the Uintah, Ouray, Southern and Ute Mountain reservations.

The school got off to a rough start, as personnel were tough and the living conditions mean. A change of staff was welcomed, and the students got down to some real learning. They engaged in home economics, sports (producing a couple of top athletes), manual labor skills, trades, farming, music and arts, as well as practical subjects like math and English.

Despite the white man's best efforts, some Indians just didn't want to be "Americanized." Escapes were not all that common, but the *News* reported them as quite colorful adventures, as in this article from June 4, 1887:

> *Indian School* ESCAPE*…Commissioner Lane has a grievance with a great big "G." Last week when the four Indians left the school without leave, they struck for the Book Cliffs, where the signal fire could be plainly seen and where were waiting six braves from the reservation to escort their brothers from school back to their native wilds. They camped the same night, ten in all, on the summit near the Book Cliff coal mines, and killed one of Mr. Lane's calves for supper. They left early next day and were seen by Mr. F.L. Whitaker, who on interviewing the truants, was informed that, "School no good. White man go to school. Indian no like. Only stay* [three] *sleeps at school."*

## Fire Escape

This story involves two thieves, a fire and the shortest time in custody recorded here. It's a good possibility that Al Paff, who was preparing for a large horse auction, lost his property to arson. His Livestock Emporium, on Ute near Third, had a sizeable arena, from where he rented out buggies and stabled horses. The night of February 18, 1889, his sheds out back caught on fire and consumed the entire business.

Water was limited, so frantic horses and wooden conveyances on site were corralled and moved to safety. All survived but three horses, which were stuck in the barn and perished in the blaze.

At the same time, the eastern-bound train was preparing to leave from the depot a couple of blocks away from the fire. Passengers were assembling, and those on board returned to their seats as the "All aboard!" sounded. A salesman approached his seat and discovered his valise was gone. Distressed, he asked around and learned that two disreputable men had been seen close by. He searched the train until he found them. After accusing them of theft, he grabbed their collars and held tight, calling for help. A Mr. Lynch asked that the train be held while he went uptown to get the city marshal.

The marshal arrived, and the salesman continued his hold while the lawman scoured the greasewood along the tracks. A triumphant shout went up when he found it. Happiness was short-lived, as the news of Paff's emporium fire finally reached the depot and caused such excitement that the hooligans slipped from their captor's grasp and got away. As the train pulled away, the salesman made sure he had a good grip on his valise.

## BATHTUB BREAK

The *Grand Junction News* article took great pains to describe the county jail from which Joseph Davis, "one of the burglars who broke into the store of John Vaughn some weeks ago," escaped on October 30, 1891. He'd been awaiting the next district court term.

Davis had friends on the outside, but he didn't need their help that night to escape. He had a plan. Sheriff Cramer's jail was laid out with an office, a kitchen and a divided steel cage. The cage was large enough for a corridor and several small cells. At the end of the corridor was a bathtub. Deputy Sheriff Smith was in charge of the three prisoners, and on the night of October 30, he went to the jail to lock them up.

During the day, they were let out in the corridor "for exercise," and then at dusk they went to their cells. On this night, the lamp in the corridor was apparently so dim that Smith couldn't see the prisoners all that well, but he thought everyone was secure and left.

What was really transpiring in the dimness was that Davis had hidden in the bathtub until Smith turned his back, and then Davis shadowed him out of the cage. He then quietly climbed on top of the cage. When Smith left the jail, Davis climbed down and escaped.

The next morning, a manhunt was on, but he was long gone. They found in the nearby sagebrush some tools, including a sledgehammer and crowbar. Obviously, Davis's friends had been on hand in case his plan didn't work.

## *Chapter 4*

# Prohibition Punch

*City jail prisoners are to be put to work on the streets. There is nothing like hard work to make a bootlegger pay his fine and do his time and then get back to his business.*

*—Al Look,* Daily Sentinel, *December 11, 1928*

Though written with a twinkle in his eye, this quotation from Al Look wasn't far off the mark. It took more than a little work to stem the flow of illegal liquor on the Western Slope, and even then, the best they got was a slow leak. Anti-saloon sentiment had been brewing for decades. One fell either into the dry or wet camp. The Woman's Christian Temperance Union and vociferous preachers spoke through meetings, the newspapers and from pulpits on the dangers of drinking, hoping to convince fence-sitters that dry was the only good choice. Once in a while, the waterfall of views was stemmed by an ordinary person's silent but powerful message.

In 1887, Fruita citizens were wrestling with whether or not to support a saloon. It was a young town with mostly dry sentiments. Independence Day came around, and one eccentric old man decided it was time to take a stand. His angst started when he'd inherited a beautiful mahogany bar slated for a saloon in Fruita. The saloon was never built, for which he was thankful, but now that bar was a bur under his saddle.

On the morning of July 5, neighbors around Van Bronk Park (today's Circle Park) awoke to quite a sight. The accursed bar squatted in the park, adorning the scruffy turf. A couple of lanky beer bottles waited by an empty glass, "suggestive and inviting enough to any old toper."

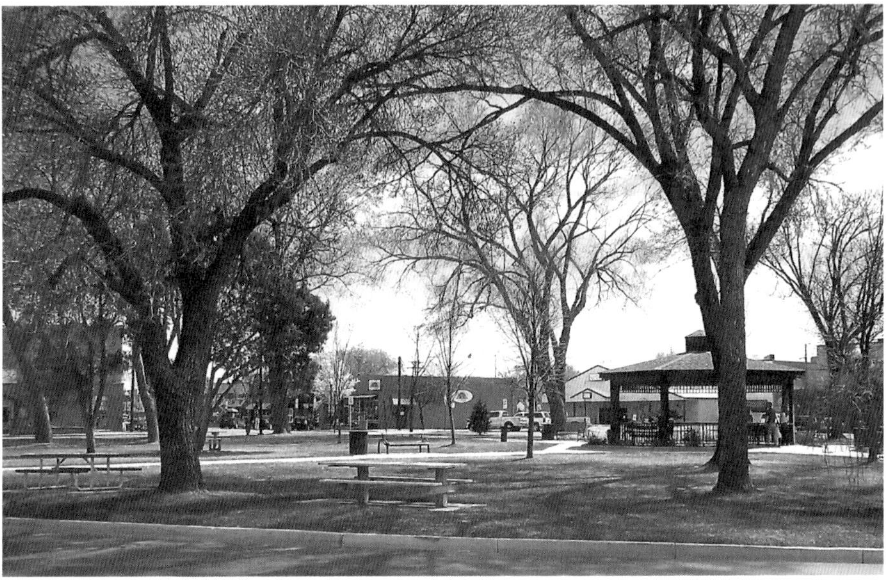

Steve and Denise Hight, Fruita historians, checked on the history of "Von Bronk" park, alluded to in the *Grand Junction News* article. It was originally named for J.P. Bronk, a Denver businessman. The consensus is he must have contributed funds to the little town, and they named the park after him. He never lived there. The park didn't carry his name for long. Originally it was square, but when a wide roundabout was installed, the park was carved to fit the new shape, and Circle Park was born. *Courtesy of Steve Henderson.*

All day, queries eddied around. Who had done this…and why? Come evening, "a tall form walked with faltering step," an axe clutched in his hand. He approached the bar and raised his arm. Soon, the offense was a pile of kindling. The old man eloquently struck a match and flicked it into the pile. Bright flames illuminated "the entire valley." Standing alone, he watched the fire until it had ebbed to embers. Then he shoveled dirt over it. A crowd watched silently to the very end. It was a long time before a saloon was established in Fruita.

The first saloon in Grand Junction was opened on December 14, 1881, by Giles and Garland. At midnight on April 18, 1909, Grand Junction went dry—eleven years before the nation did. For the first time in twenty-eight years, there was no place to whet your whistle. Thus began the most illustrious chase the Western Slope has ever known: law versus bootleggers.

The dry citizens were jubilant at the turn of events, but not everyone was ready to fold. There was a run on the drinking houses that last wet day, like nothing they'd ever seen. Nine thirst houses and Maurice Hertz's wholesale liquor distributorship were picked clean.

On the morning of December 18, several saloons had transformed into soft drink parlors. Owners put on a good face of propriety, but everyone knew that underneath the bar rug was a nice cache of beer, wine and harder spirits, ready to be dispensed at the right word.

Grand Junction's administration had just changed, and they were adamant that their arrest record be pristine. Knowing their constituents may need some time to adjust to the "dry" climate, the police were told to ignore infractions for a time. Law-abiding citizens became a tad curious when a drunk collapsed at a lawman's feet and he simply stepped over him. Merchant policeman Andy Halligan could only take so much of that nonsense. Three weeks into imposed sanctions, "a man superbly drunk and emphatic in his hilarity" was arrested by Halligan and dragged to jail. The next day, he appeared in court and was found guilty. He received a charge of five dollars, plus costs. Halligan received a dressing down and almost lost his job over his impetuousness.

When the home supply started to dwindle, the fun began. It was common knowledge that drugstores carried "medicinal" spirits, and when

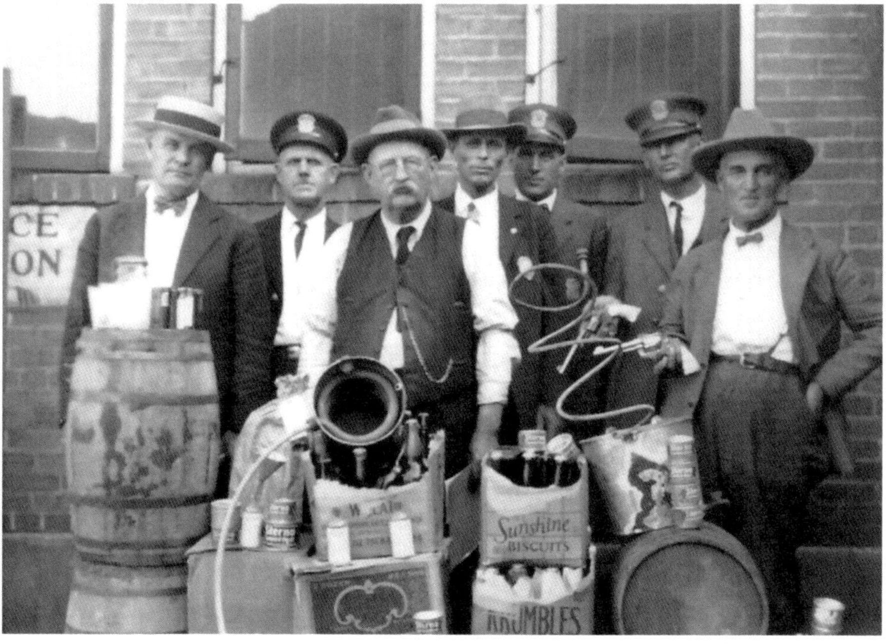


Police Chief H.E. Decker and his force were kept busy finding and destroying stills during Prohibition. Notice the barred windows of the police station and the meager fastenings on the outside windows. This haul is big enough to have been the booty after a citywide raid. The officer second from the left is Dorothy Doyle's father, Culver Harris. *Courtesy of Dorothy Doyle.*

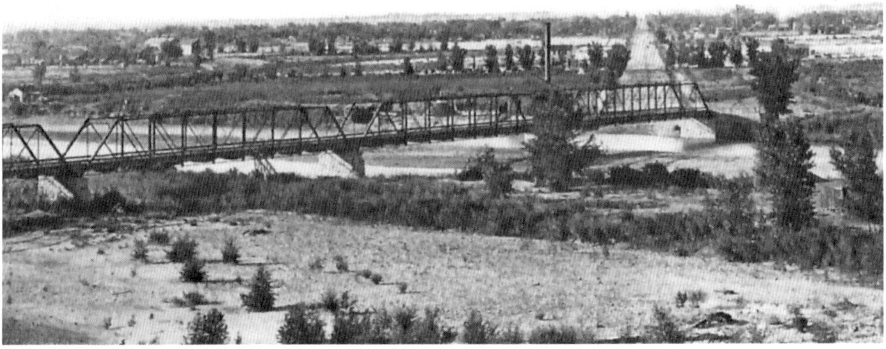

The Fifth Street Bridge was the first bridge in the valley. Built in 1886, it was the longest bridge in Colorado at the time. It was replaced in 1933 and then again in the 1980s. It overshadows the Colorado River, originally named the Grand River. Before the bridge, people crossed the river via ferryboats, a very precarious way to travel, especially in late spring, when the river roared with snowmelt. Many a drowning occurred the first year or so. *Courtesy of Loyd Files Research Library.*

men got thirsty, these became targets. The first victim was Wohlfort Drug. The crook or crooks blithely bypassed counters displaying jewelry on the way back to the storage rooms. Giddiness surely turned sour when it was discovered that there were no spirits. The *News* mused about this and also wondered what they were planning to do with the two hatchets they stole. The next day, Van Horn Drugs was broken into in broad daylight. Again, nothing was found. Only two drugstores in town carried medicinal spirits, and these two weren't them. You better believe the others shored up their stores from then on.

Soon, stills began production, operating in Glade Park, Coates and Roan Creeks, in Ouray, De Beque and on Little Park Road, near Grand Junction. The police were kept hopping finding and destroying them. The fish in the Grand (Colorado) River must have been drunk continuously with all the booze that was dumped at the Fifth Street Bridge.

Prohibition turned some good men bad and bad men badder. Wives became liars as they testified that their men were with them when, in fact, they'd been to the still. The courts became more and more skeptical of these tales and locked the suspects behind bars just on principle. The jails became crammed with bootleggers, and finally, out of desperation, the masses were simply fined (or put to work on the streets) and sent home.

## Abe Wrong

Abe C. Ong was the poster child for moonshine. The prolific "pioneer bootlegger" lived in De Beque and also had a home at Third and Ute in Grand Junction. He kept the judge busy for a decade, but his cases were constantly being thrown out of court because of a ridiculous technicality: if evidence was brought to the sheriff, he could use it against Ong, but he wasn't allowed to go get it himself. Since half the county relied on Ong and his endless supply of booze, it was rare when someone ratted him out. He wasn't impervious, though.

In August 1911, Ong was finally convicted of selling liquor "indiscriminately" and sentenced to five months in the county jail. He also received a $500 fine plus costs. He was one of twenty-five bootleggers arrested from the De Beque area.

Certain county citizens thought the sheriff was doing a lousy job where De Beque was concerned. It practically bubbled over with bootleggers.

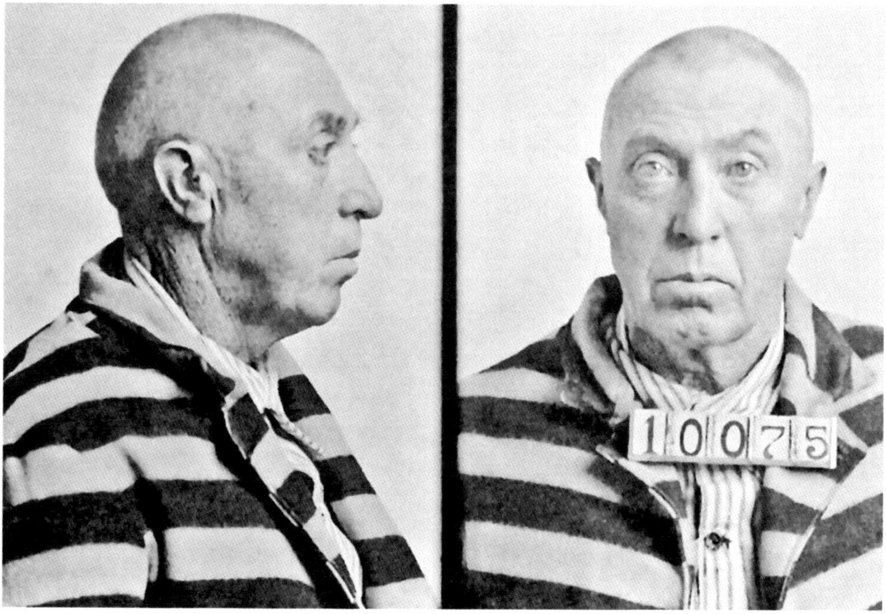


Abe Ong was the most prolific of the Western Slope's plethora of bootleggers. His father was a judge in Grand Junction, though he wasn't acknowledged as so, and probably for good reason. Born in Illinois, Ong and his family moved to the Roan Creek–De Beque area. He may have begun his life of crime when he worked at a De Beque saloon. After his incarcerations, he moved to Leadville, where he is listed in the 1930 census as seventy years old. *Courtesy of Colorado State Archives.*

The *Grand Junction News* criticized Sheriff Schrader, partly because he was a Republican and they were Democrat, but it also wondered if maybe there wasn't something underhanded going on.

A year after Ong's August 1911 trial, the *Sentinel* reported that the *News* had sent a reporter named Emmett Fuller to De Beque undercover. They accused the "Republican bull moose paper" of seeking evidence that bootlegging thrived there so its man, William Struthers, could get elected for sheriff in the upcoming election. The *Sentinel* editor assured "the morning press agent of the wet candidate for sheriff" that Sheriff Charles Schrader was not turning a blind eye to bootlegging. His hands were bound because of the law.

Fuller "disguised" himself as a "detective" and allied himself with the "bums, who knew the ropes." Contrary to the rumor that whiskey careened down the streets of De Beque, it took twenty-four hours for Fuller to finally purchase some hooch. Fuller's excuse for why it took so long was that the man who usually sold whiskey was out of town. Turns out that the "man" was Abe Ong, who'd been in jail under five indictments for bootlegging. When he got back "in town," he sold Fuller his bottle.

The *Sentinel* was jubilant of the outcome but scathing in its remarks toward the reporter and his boss. Perhaps public opinion forced his actions, or his typographical union blackballed his tactics as "violating union principles by doing detective work for political reasons," but Fuller resigned.

Ong continued his unsavory career. Just before Valentine's Day 1914, he was arrested as part of a sting that netted five other bootleggers. In 1915, a bottle-busting party down by the river destroyed some of Abe Ong's best brew.

In 1916, a raid on a millinery store, several soft drink establishments and the usual bootleggers yielded a combined team of law enforcement plenty. Among them, and "in that no raid of the bootlegging element would be considered complete without [Ong] figuring in it in some way," Abe Ong and his assistant, George "Peg Leg" Slutis, were arrested. A thorough search of these places revealed creative hiding places for the booze, including underneath a sleeping baby in a perambulator, within a sewing machine and beneath a pile of coal in a backyard.

A year later, Ong was back in court with a packed gallery as he was found guilty again. Three undercover scouts had bought liquor at Ong's Third and Pitkin "place of business." It was argued that this was really his residence and that he had a right to keep liquor there for his own use. Ong's attorney called no witnesses, and this slim defense led to a guilty verdict. Ong did two stints in the Colorado penal system.

By 1924, the newspapers regularly reported the arrests of bootleggers, capturing of stills and disposing of goods. Once in a while, the police were involved in wild goose chases. On May 21, 1924, two arrested bootleggers from Ouray escaped their captors, stole a car and barreled toward Grand Junction. The cops stayed close behind them, losing ground when they stopped to retrieve liquor bottles thrown out the car windows.

Grand Junction chief of police Bert Watson and several others took the baton and posted themselves at the Whitewater bridge. Standing in front of the barricade they built, they waited confidently for the approaching car. As the headlights grew larger, it became apparent that the boys weren't going to stop. The sentinels jumped out of the way as the runners broke through the barricade, showering the air with wood splinters. They were still dumping booty, and more than thirty gallons were collected afterward. The automobile disappeared from sight, headlights piercing the darkness. Early the next day, their wrecked car was found in the Gunnison River, minus the men.

## Palisade Prevails

> *There was a lively mixup on the Colorado Midland train today...the principles being Harold Stevens, the detective who has been working on the Palisade liquor cases, and Mrs. Ferguson, wife of one of the defendants... According to witnesses...Mrs. Ferguson had a rather vigorous interview with Mr. Stevens...When Stevens left her...Mrs. Ferguson followed and proceeded to give Stevens a drubbing with her umbrella. Mayor Reeder and others interfered...Mr. Stevens went out on the platform and Mr. Reeder held the door closed until the train stopped.*
>
> *Then Mrs. Ferguson pursued Stevens across the depot platform until he took refuge in the St. Regis Hotel. A woman friend of Mrs. Ferguson then took her...out of the "war zone."*
>
> —Daily Sentinel, *March 10, 1911*

William Donovan, Palisade's town marshal, did his best to combat bootlegging in his neck of the woods. Drunks were arrested, and bootleggers were convicted. James Ferguson had done some time for both infractions, but that hadn't deterred him from continuing.

On July 4, 1911, he and William Price and another man took exception to Donovan when he tried to arrest them for drunkenness in front of Mayor

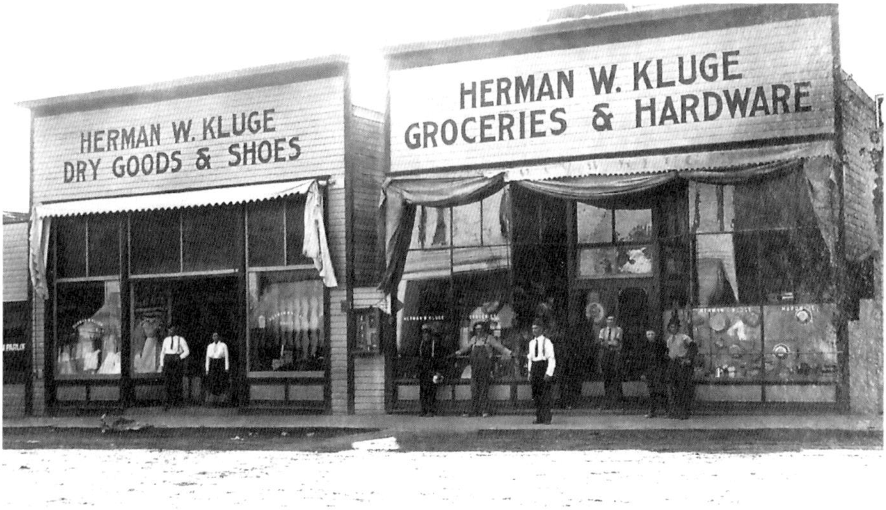


Palisade is world-famous for its incredible peaches and now its wines. Vineyards were nonexistent during Prohibition, however. Of German descent, Herman W. Kluge built up his business in the east end of the Grand Valley. His general merchandise store claimed it was a "dealer in a little of everything." Eventually, he was elected the first mayor of Palisade, and he has a street named after him. *Courtesy of Loyd Files Research Library and Priscilla Walker.*

Kluge's store. Ferguson "hit [Donavon] with all his might a number of terrific blows in the face and shoulder" while his two companions held him. The lawman crumpled to the ground, and they ran over the bridge and into the trees, toward the coal mines above the town.

Donovan was put to bed while an impassioned search took place, but the men weren't found. Later, they returned to town and were arrested. The *Sentinel* reminded the readers of Mrs. Ferguson's attack on a detective earlier in the year. This didn't help the mood of the town.

A week later, anger found its voice. "A secret and determined mob of night riders" mustered around Ferguson's restaurant in Palisade. About seventy-five "heavily masked" marauders brandished shotguns and revolvers. The "stealthy tread of feet and the low sharp commands of a leader were heard," scaring Ferguson's night crew.

Two young boys were forced at gunpoint to deliver a typewritten message to J.M. and Charles Ferguson, as well as to the owner of a chili parlor across the street, E.B. Reynolds:

> *Warning to James M. Ferguson: Within ten days from July 10th, 1911, you MUST close your business, and take your family and leave this TOWN*

> *and NOT return. You will be dealt with AT ONCE for any insult, abuse, or violence by yourself or wife towards any citizen of this TOWN during the ten (10) days. GET BUSY.*

It was signed "Law and Order League."

News traveled like the wind, and soon the entire Western Slope was wringing its hands with worry and excitement. An emergency session of the Palisade town council met, and Attorney Rozzelle spoke on behalf of the Fergusons, asking for protection. One irritated alderman remarked that they had one constable and reminded Rozzelle that his client had beat him up. Cooler heads assured Rozzelle that protection would be given in some way. Mayor Kluge made a statement the next day that this would be followed up and dealt with and that he didn't believe any harm would come to the group, "IF THE MEN LEAVE AS ORDERED."

Ferguson cited that he had property in the valley and couldn't just up and leave it. He said he knew who some of the marauders were, including a certain man of the cloth. "We're not afraid of their night riders," he proclaimed. "Let them come out openly."

Sheriff Schrader insisted there would be no mob violence forthcoming, and this was reiterated when Governor of Colorado John F. Shaforth wrote the sheriff that he must "prevent mob violence at any cost." One of the threatened, E.B. Reynolds, had sent a copy of the warning to the governor.

The *Sentinel* "set its foot against mob law" in a July 11, 1911 editorial. It had savory words for law enforcement, too: "The Fergusons should have been made to respect and obey the law…if the authorities had to arrest each and every one of them every day in the year."

As the deadline approached, J.M. and Charles Ferguson disappeared. Their businesses were "in other hands," and even though the Mistresses Ferguson were still in town, they said they would be joining their husbands soon. Mr. Reynolds insisted he wasn't going to be run out of town. The governor's order to protect him no matter what had "quieted" the night riders.

The defendants were afraid they'd not get a fair trial in Palisade, so their hearing, on July 13, 1911, was held in the bank building in Clifton, in Justice Shriver's court. The timid Clifton citizens were afraid the mob would rise up again and asked for a police presence, which was granted.

Since the Fergusons were a no-show, their $500 bond, paid for by William Price, was forfeited, and the jury heard the case against Price for assaulting Marshal Donavon. Price was convicted of assault and sentenced to six months in the county jail. He requested a new trial.

## STRAIGHT SHOTS

*Some precious citizen burglarized the Corner Saloon one night* [two weeks prior] *and carried away about $200 worth of liquors and cigars. They seemed to consider it safe to deposit their ill gotten stock on the banks of the river, but were soon discovered and taken to jail by Sheriff Cramer. The men who robbed the Corner Saloon last week, imbibed so much they burned themselves badly on their camp fire. One burned his leg and foot nearly to the bone.*
—Grand Junction News, *December 21, 1889*

*Buried in the hay under a setting hen in a chicken house, Chief of Police Wallis yesterday afternoon found several bottles of whisky. What mental process led him to uncover the booze in the secret hiding place is a mystery to his friends, but unquestionably he has qualified as a sleuth by his act.*
—Daily Sentinel, *April 16, 1914*

*Snoring peacefully on the top step of the stairs of the Fair building* [at the southeast corner of Main and Fifth], *an unknown toper spent several hours this morning sleeping off the effects of some particularly bad bootleg whiskey. He appeared to have fallen while laboriously climbing the stairs and with his pipe still between his teeth, crumpled up on the rather uncomfortable bed and slipped off to slumber land.*
—Daily Sentinel, *January 14, 1911*

*The campaign in Mesa County for state-wide prohibition will open next Saturday under auspices of Mesa County Dry Colorado league when several hundred children from the various Sunday schools of the county will participate in a monster parade through the streets of the city. It is expected by the organizers of the movement that not less than 500 children will be in line carrying banners and streamers with mottoes and legends favoring the state-wide prohibition movement.*
—Daily Sentinel, *October 7, 1912*

*Obituary—William Armstrong…resided on the old Wellington place* [near Mantey Heights] *and was universally liked. His home was happy, except for strong drink drove him to the saloon. No one who knew him would for a moment have thought he would have sought self destruction, but the terrible depression which follows the protracted use of strong drink*

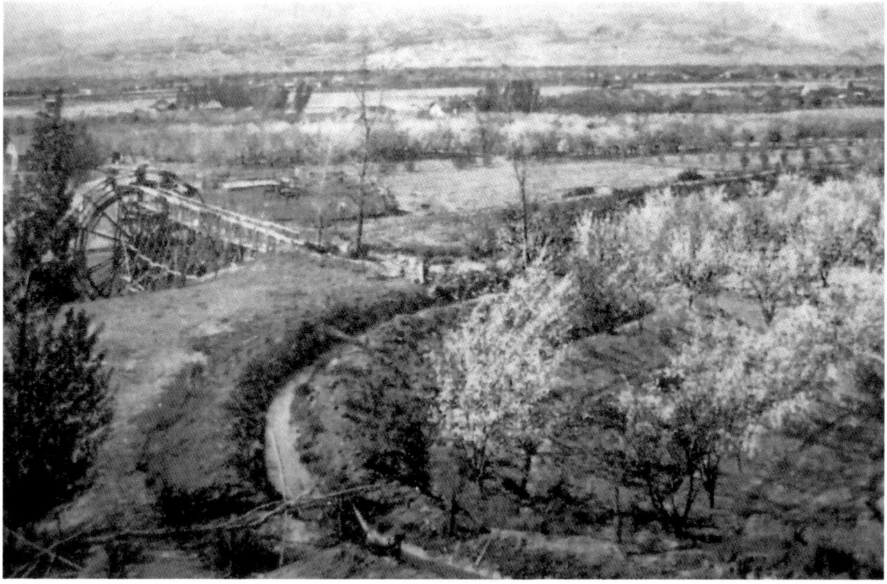

Wellington Heights was located near present-day Mantey Heights, on Patterson Road. The ranch was owned by J.A. Wellington, who had a huge water wheel built to bring water up from the big ditch at the end of Seventeenth Street. After he died, his widow married William Armstrong, and again she was widowed. Fred Mantey bought Wellington's hilltop property around 1909 and developed Mantey Heights. *Author's collection.*

> *was too much for him to withstand, and on Wednesday morning he fired the shot into his brain which finally resulted in his death.*
> —Grand Junction News, *May 20, 1905*

As if there wasn't enough trouble locally, one time a traveling Kickapoo medicine show had set up its tents on Main Street. After the afternoon theatrics, one of the actors imbibed a little too much of his company's "medicine" and jumped out of his second-story hotel window when he thought the room was on fire. The town marshal was happy to see the back end of the wagons growing distant.

And then there was this tidbit in the *Grand Junction Daily Sentinel*, dated July 1, 1928: "Ordinarily when a man is behind prison bars, he is safe from the temptation of the cup that cheers, but this failed to be true of a Mexican arrested Friday night for intoxication and lodged in the calaboose to sleep off his jag." He didn't show up for his hearing the next morning, and a search party was sent out. They found him in his cell, still drunk—if not more so—loudly singing songs of his homeland. A thorough investigation led to the discovery of a batch of moonshine that was scheduled for disposal fermenting just a foot from the man's reach. He'd joyfully partaken of this surprising gift. The liquor was promptly removed, and the happy gent was allowed another day to recuperate before meeting the judge.

## *Chapter 5*

# Red All Over

Very little is mentioned in the first years regarding brothels. When they did make the news, they were given sobriquets like bawdy or sporting houses and houses of ill repute. In 1882, when Mike Dunn was shot and killed by Marshal Crowley at a saloon, Kitty Sheedy was injured in the panic. A later recounting of this event by J. Clayton Nichols refers to Kit and her "lady friends in the same line of business," who were anxious to make a reputation for themselves.

Emma Thompson's "infamous bagino" was the site of several shooting sprees. On Sunday night, January 7, 1883, George Mosby had taken a lady to the back of the saloon where a room accommodated patrons. The only problem was that Mr. Al Turner thought she was his gal. He watched the closed door, all the while his simmering temper heating to a boil. When the gal came out to get some cigars, Turner followed her back to the door, carrying his revolver.

He called Mosby out of the room, but Mosby was not inclined to leave. Instead, he pulled out his gun and shot twice, one ball striking Turner in the cheek. It exited near his right ear. The second shot went over his head as Turner fell through the thin wall of the restaurant next door. He landed in the lap of James Wilkins, a waiter. Wilkins was wounded "severely, and it was thought he will die," according to the *Grand Junction News* of January 13, 1883.

Justice Shanks acquitted Mosby on Monday, saying it was self-defense. The *News* used this opportunity to state the obvious moral effects of saloons, brothels and the "free use of fire-arms in the hands of dangerous and reckless persons."

## 240's Sporty

It's unsure exactly when 240 Colorado was built, but by 1899, a Sanborn Fire Map shows a "female rooming" house with a kitchen to the west of the building. A 1901 *Grand Junction Daily Sentinel* article reports a "slight fire at the 240 house," which evacuated "four to six colorful women" and quite a few "guests." They milled around the street, along with a "great crowd of men and boys" who had appeared out of nowhere. The flames were quickly doused, but it took a while for interest to die down.

In 1901, the *Grand Junction Daily Sentinel* relayed the story of the silk peddler who got taken by a couple of 240 ladies. Mr. Allison usually had his chest of silks carried directly from the depot when he arrived, to whichever "sporting" house (or houses) was in town. Allison had conducted his business and had his chest hauled back to the depot by porter Albert Brown and rode the rails to Glenwood Springs. When he opened his chest there, he discovered he'd been robbed. Quickly, he ran to the depot and jumped on the next train back to Grand Junction to file a complaint. Brown was the first suspect, and he was arrested. A search of his home, though, garnered no evidence. He was released, but later, because he was "acting suspiciously," the unfortunate man was rearrested. When the authorities learned that two of 240's women had taken the train to Utah, they concluded that the women had stolen the goods. Not much sympathy was generated for the peddler, though. His prices were exorbitant, and the general feeling was that a robber had gotten a bit of his own.

Hundreds of fights and "at least" one murder transpired at that "moral sore spot" over the years. Most Grand Junction citizens chose to ignore the little house of ill repute on Colorado Avenue. It persisted through various movements to remove the notorious "resort." One such push came in the fall of 1906, and it was hopeful that this one would stick. The *News* heralded, "The business district of Grand Junction, at least, will be purged of the unsightly resort, and its painted inmates will have to flock to some other haven to pluck their victims."

This particular maneuver stemmed from a knife fight between two of Madam Grace Winford's inmates, Fern and Effie. They'd been arguing for weeks, and it culminated in Fern beating Effie on the head with brass knuckles and Effie stabbing Fern several times. "Miss Fern" was at the hospital and was not expected to live through the night, while Effie sweated out her fate. Fern survived, as did the movement to close 240.

On October 1, 1904, Grace Winford was shut down. For a time, anyway. A year later, another arrest flustered the population. In October 1907, Wang Fu was arrested for running an ill-governed house in association with

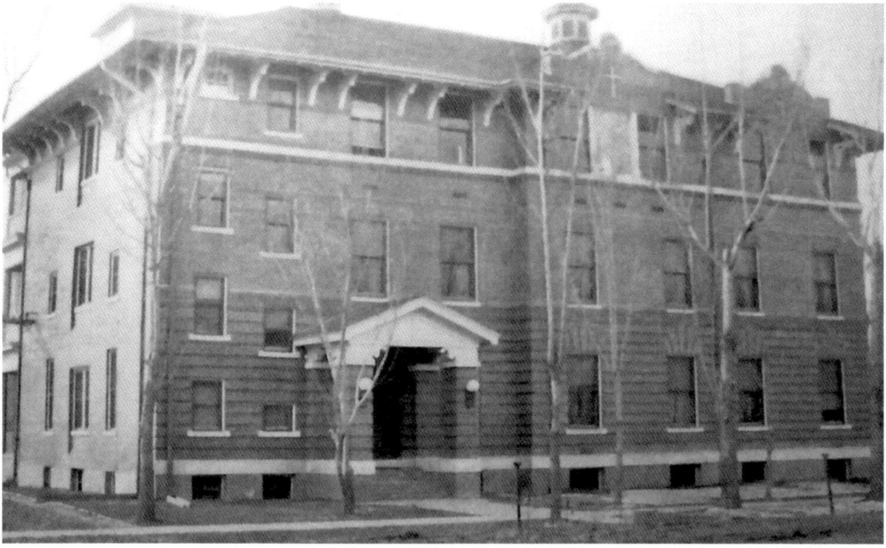

St. Mary's Hospital was built in 1896 by the Sisters of Charity of Leavenworth. Located on Colorado Avenue between Eleventh and Twelfth Streets, it had ten beds and four sisters to take care of patients. It was welcomed in town, as hospitals had come and gone, and now it looked like one was here to stay. St. Mary's now towers at the top of Seventh Street, a state-of-the-art full-service hospital complex. *Author's collection.*

his "Noodle restaurant" just west of 240 Colorado. He was charged with allowing young boys to act unseemly with women and drink beer in his establishment. He was outraged at the charges.

The district alderman met with the city council in December and adjured them to rid the neighborhood of 240, which was "greatly disturbing" the neighbors.

The last madam of 240 was Kathryn Hunter (aka Kathryn Stone). When longtime citizen Jessie Sperber was a child, she often was called to dance for the ladies in her parlor. Jessie never saw anything unseemly. Kathryn was a generous woman, too. She often slipped money into pockets without her beneficiaries knowing it. When she became old, those whom she had helped came to her assistance.

The establishment had an enduring quality, and despite many stringent attempts by the authorities and religious people, 240 remained ensconced on Colorado Avenue until the 1940s, when Kathryn died. She willed her house to her lawyer, Scott W. Heckman.

According to Charlie Traylor, who inventoried the house, there were drawers full of silk stockings—illegal during World War II—which Kathryn sold to customers. Beautiful stained glass, marble tabletops and high-end furnishings graced the rooms. A three- by four-inch framed nude photo that hung on one wall was sold to Telluride's New Sheridan Motel for its bar, and it still resides there. The illustrious, long-lived house was at last torn down for a parking lot.

Several red-light neighborhoods sprung up over the first half century of the town's existence. Shanties on Colorado Avenue, between First and Second Streets, transformed into Grand Junction's version of the "Barbary Coast." In 1907, 119 Colorado Avenue, originally the first "hospital" run by Mary Briley, housed two women and two men. None were related. They were arrested on Saturday night, May 4, charged with running a disorderly house. The *Grand Junction News* headlined a May 6, 1907 article: "High Old Time This Morning When Colored 'Soiled Angels' Told Their Tales."

On Monday morning, the foursome appeared before Judge Hill and a packed gallery. The complaining witness proclaimed that he'd recently seen a fight between the two gals, and they were hurling "delicious epithets" at each other. The editors of the newspaper hurled a few of their own in their unflattering and crude descriptions of the two ladies standing trial. When it was their turn to speak, each shared that they tried to be ladies and earn their living honestly and that they did not run a disorderly house. In between pleas of innocence, they sent "many a dangerous look" to the complaining witness.

The *News* states, "At times the court proceedings got very lively indeed." The women were found guilty and fined the typical five dollars plus costs.

The southeast corner of Second and Colorado was home to the Royalty Club saloon, and right behind it was another "female boarding" house. That place tried its luck as a red-light destination, but Lucille, who ran the "ill-governed" house, didn't have the stomach for the legal accoutrements that went with the business. Late in 1907, Lucille was arrested. She pled guilty and said she'd move out of town right away.

## Murdered Twice, Not Nice

Hob-legged madam Mrs. Jennie Ward provided gambling and prostitution for the railroad men. The Barbary Coast became famous for two murders, one in 1937 and the other in 1954. Jeanette Morris, who had worked only a short time for Mrs. Ward as a chauffeur and housekeeper, was murdered on August 13, 1937. Found by Mrs. Ward early the next morning, the young mother was strewn half-naked across her bed with an apron string tied tightly

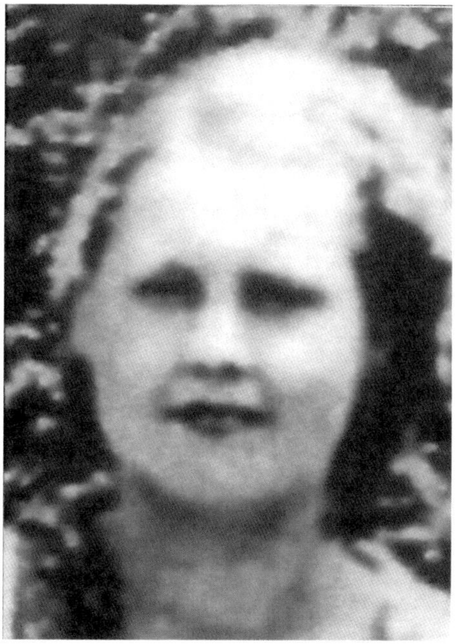

Jeanette Morris was the mother of a four-year-old boy when she was murdered around midnight on Friday, August 13, 1937. In the Polk 1937 city directory, she was listed as housekeeper at 133 Colorado Avenue, a position she held for six weeks. As she worked for the madam of the Barbary Coast, she was incorrectly labeled a prostitute herself. This reputation followed her family like a black cloud for over a half century. Later, her murder was sensationalized in detective magazines. *Courtesy of Thelma Liggett.*

around her neck. Two locks of hair had been snipped off her head, one lying nearby and the other missing.

This was the first in a series of sensational murders that took place in the downtown area. Special Detective Walter Byron was secured from Denver to help solve Jeanette's murder and that of Big Kid Eames in 1938. The beginning of 1939 yielded suspects for both.

Cecil McHolland was caught due to his stupidity. He was working on a farm in Pueblo and showed a picture of Jeanette, his "girlfriend," to his boss. When Cecil turned it over, the man saw a lock of hair taped to the back, and suddenly he remembered the news story about Jeanette. He called the sheriff in Mesa County, and Cecil was brought back to Grand Junction.

When they finally got a real confession from him, the details of Jeanette's last evening were told. McHolland had a crush on Jeanette, but the girl wasn't interested. He and a friend, W.D. Miller, had seen her sitting on the curb in front of the Hotel D'Hamburger at Main and Second that Friday night. She was waiting with her brother for her boyfriend, J.D. Lumpkin, to finish his shift. He was a dishwasher at the restaurant. The two men pulled up and invited her to a night of drinking. Jeanette instructed her brother, Dick Jones, to tell J.D. that she was sick and going home. She got in the car, and that was the last time she was seen alive by her loved ones.

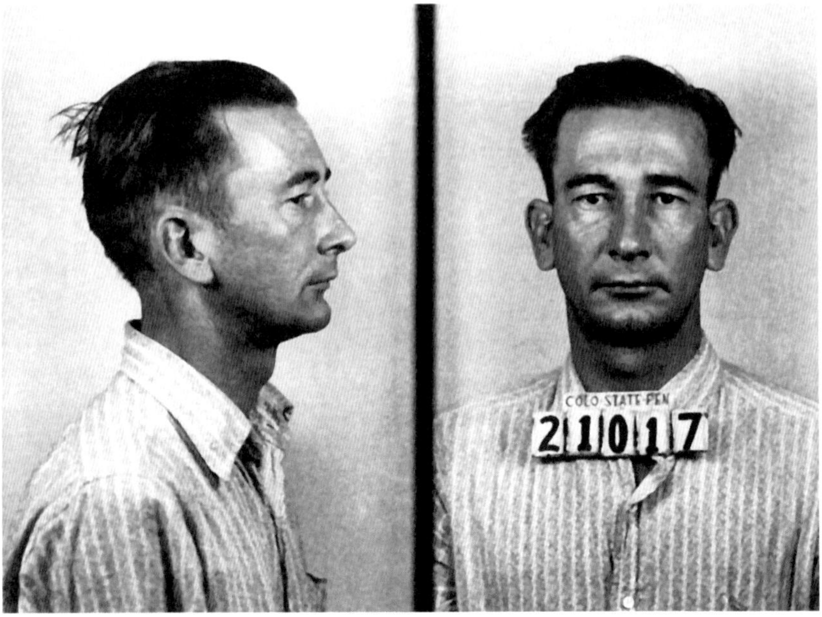


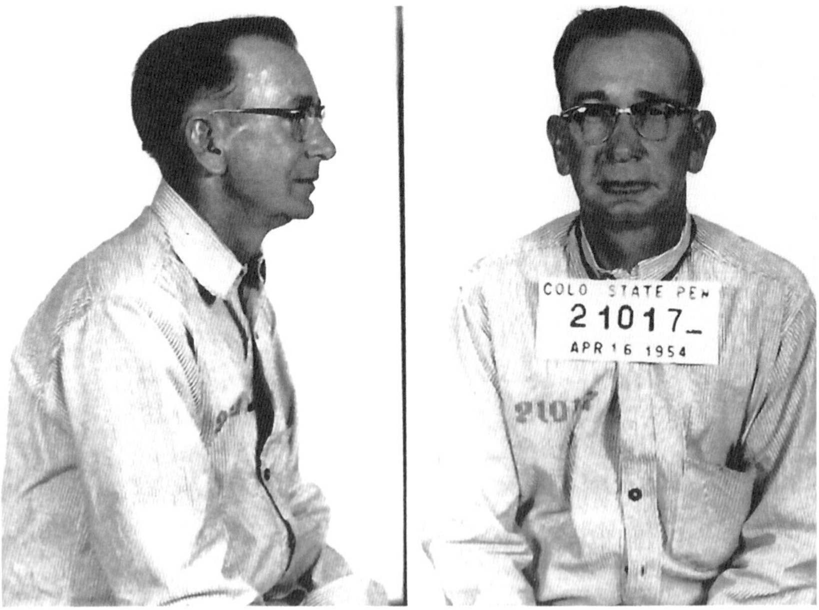


*This page*: Cecil McHolland, a married man with a newborn child, ruined his life by pursuing love outside of marriage. That, combined with too much drink and a jealous streak, wound him up in jail for twenty years. By the time he was released in 1954, when a parole board decided he hadn't killed Jeanette Morris, he had only six more years to live. His grandchildren and family remember very little of him, and the only epitaph they have of him is the whispered, "He killed a girl." *Courtesy of Colorado State Archives.*

It's possible that Jeanette was murdered twice in one night, with evidence pointing to Cecil McHolland beginning the process and Mrs. Ward finishing it. Two things point to this. During the trial, McHolland and Miller confessed that a jealous and drunken McHolland throttled Jeanette into unconsciousness in her shanty at 133 Colorado. But they believed she was alive when they left. McHolland had shaken her with his hands, and finger bruises on her neck attested to that. However, they were located *under* the apron strings. Both men denied that an apron ever entered the fracas.

Jeanette's brother tried to tell the authorities that Jeanette was afraid of Mrs. Ward. She'd found out the madam was involved in white slavery and believed she was next in line. Hurriedly, she looked for another job. The day she died, she'd put in an application at the Hotel D'Hamburger. Why this testimony was ignored is curious, but it was never brought up in court.

Despite the apron string discrepancy, McHolland was found guilty of murder in the first degree and sentenced to life in prison. He was sent to Canon City. Miller was acquitted of his charges, and Mrs. Ward continued her work.

In 1954, a parole board decided, after reviewing the evidence, that McHolland hadn't gotten a fair trial and likely hadn't actually killed Jeanette. He was released from prison, and he went back to his hometown in Oklahoma. He died of a heart attack six years later.

Mrs. Ward died in the 1940s. After the murder of Artieba Dirdon in 1954, the city got serious about removing the unsightly blot from the downtown area. It was razed to the ground, and the entire block was occupied by a brand-new motel.

## That's Some Bad Mother!

Madams selling their girls into slavery wasn't an unusual pastime. Abhorrent as it is, "soiled doves" were thought of as chattel. Not that the girls understood this. They were enamored with the promise of a beautiful wardrobe, quick money and escape from their tortured lives.

Alice Baine took advantage of their hard luck stories. Said to be sister to Kathryn Stone, of 240 fame, she'd worked in a millinery shop in Denver for years and then made corsets. Around 1917, she took over 550 South Avenue, in Grand Junction, continuing its line of work. She and a partner ran another large brothel in Denver. The building at 550 South Avenue was a two-story house with a dance hall and attached garage. It

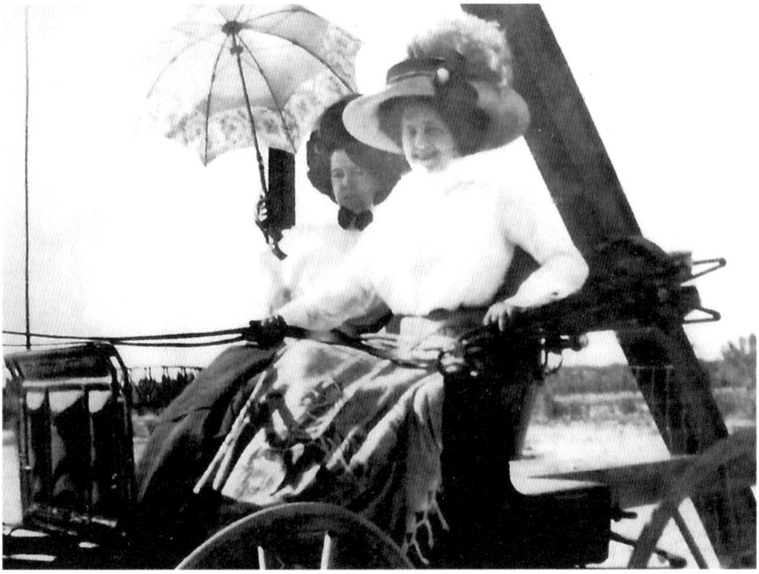

"Broken Jaw" Nell, seated on the left of the horse-drawn buggy, ran a bawdyhouse at 538 South Avenue—"the Row." Jean Harris, next to her, was her neighbor and fellow madam. Nellie Page was disfigured, reportedly from a shooting in a Leadville saloon, and always wore a high collar. The madams were known around town for their generosity, though generally no one acknowledged knowing them. *Courtesy of Loyd Files Research Library.*

was one of several bawdyhouses that made up "the Row." It was built in 1904, and its construction brought madam Pearl Miller to court. The contractor had suspicions, due to the layout of the house, that it would harbor prostitutes. Consequently, Pearl was accused of being an "inmate of a bawdy house." She pled not guilty. When she appeared before Justice Byers, the courtroom was "crowded to suffocation by men, women, and some pretty young boys." Justice Byers was criticized later for allowing the large crowd, as well as the hearty applause, which "surely affected the jury." Attorney Samuel Wheeler attacked the ministers who brought the case, and "Biblical quotations flew thick and fast." The jury brought in a verdict of not guilty, and the Row was birthed.

One day, the morning news shocked residents of Denver and Grand Junction. On May 13, 1928—Mother's Day—Mrs. Alice Baine was arrested at 2303 Curtis Street, a hotel, along with the manager of the hotel, who was Baine's partner, Bee Howard. They were charged with vice and human trafficking. Revealed in the report was that Baine, who'd "more or less openly" run 550 South Avenue for many years, was also the ringleader of a white slavery ring that operated in Colorado, New Mexico, Utah and Wyoming.

The two women were caught in a sting by the United Investigation Bureau, which had sent in a pretty young agent to pretend a desire to go into the business. Alice was impressed. She said when interviewing Miss Lita Steward, "We like baby-faced girls, not too plump." She encouraged Lita to let her "bob" grow until it touched her shoulders and promised her a life of luxury in Grand Junction. An arrangement was made, and after a switch at the train station, Baine and Howard were arrested. S. Solomon, a Denver jeweler, posted Alice's bail.

That wasn't the last of the sensation. Several days later, the *Sentinel* reported that Hazel Daniels, a former inmate of 550 South Avenue, said she'd been sold into slavery by Alice Baine. What made her case extraordinary was that Mrs. Baine was her own mother. She claimed her mother had been dealing

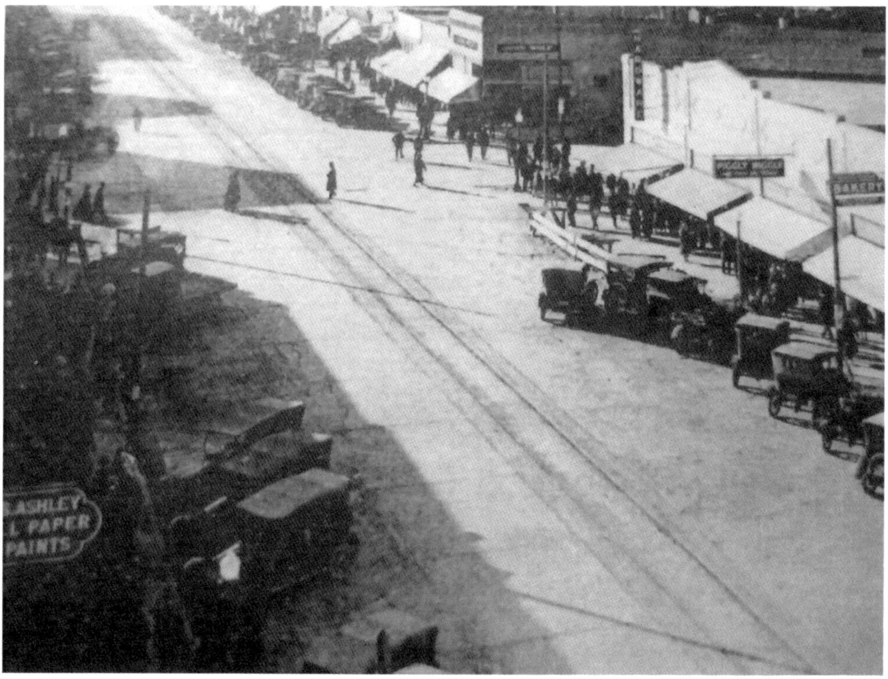

The Roaring Twenties in Grand Junction were about the same as in the rest of the world. Economy was burgeoning, with the Model T becoming affordable to the general population. New technology filled store shelves with the latest must-have gadgets, and fashion and music were heaving the Victorian generation over in their graves. The government was pushing for better hygiene, improved medicine and home improvement. *Courtesy of Loyd Files Research Library.*

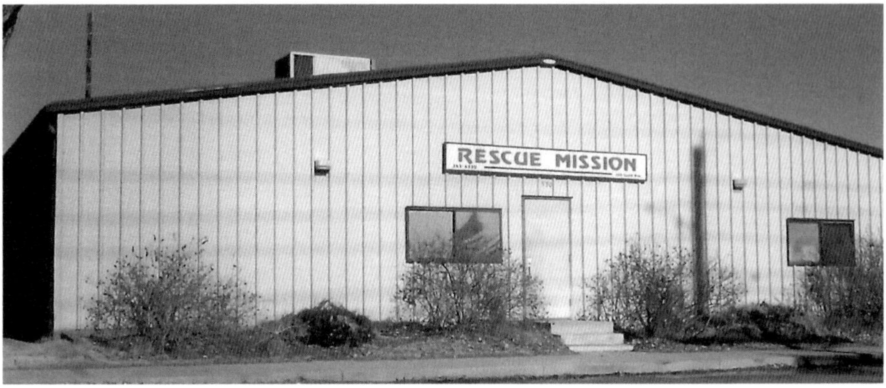


There were at least four houses of ill repute on South Avenue between Fifth and Sixth Streets. The most notorious house was 550 South Avenue, run by Alice Baine. Today, where it used to stand is a rescue mission. Two of the old brothel houses to the west are now utilized for the mission's homeless. *Author's collection.*

with young girls for almost forty years. Girls from as far away as Chicago had been enticed to join a life of shame, and the price on each head was twenty-five dollars. Baine brought the girls to Denver and then meted them out to points in Colorado and surrounding states. Hazel had spent years at 550 South Avenue before she found the courage to leave and felt it was time to speak up. Proceedings to shut down the resort began immediately.

Alice Baine was the last madam at that address. City directories list her there until 1932, after which it was turned into a reputable rooming house.

## *Chapter 6*

# Gentle Banditos

## Bridges Over Troubled Water

Is there a breaking point in every man, at which time secret temptation finally cracks the sublime veneer and consumes his world? What other explanation could explain how truly decent men, who built Grand Junction from the bottom up, fell so deeply into shame?

John W. Bridges came to Grand Junction sometime in 1883 to manage the Western Union office located within the new Denver & Rio Grande Railroad depot. He was also the train's night operator. Bridges and his wife, Lizzie, turned the office into a cozy apartment. The *News* described their walls as "artistically adorned with pictures, dados, [and] deer heads." It added that "different articles of bric a brac" were "strewn around."

Bridges jumped feet first into pioneer citizenship and ignited enthusiasm for his forward-thinking ideas. He was praised for raising funds to put up a telephone line between the depot and Main Street, the very first in town. It was equipped with a Bell telephone and could be used by the public, saving businessmen "ten to fifteen dollars worth of time every year."

When that was accomplished, Bridges moved on to electrifying the town. Up until then, gas lamps were used to illuminate, but electricity was the newest craze. Several Colorado towns were electrified, and Bridges traveled to each one, checking out their systems and trying to find the best one for his beloved town. He liked Aspen's system, which was run by water power. He believed the nearby Grand and Gunnison Rivers could provide enough power to run a plant. When the city took up the cause, he moved on to other worthy projects.

In March 1888, he was appointed president of the Grand Junction Building and Loan Company when Lucius Cost died and left the position open. Everyone thought he was the perfect choice, especially since he owned a good portion of the stock. Illness plagued the good-natured man, and he had to step down temporarily from the Western Union and depot jobs while he recuperated. Once he was well, he took up his positions again.

A Republican, Bridges was nominated for postmaster in 1889 and won. He was lauded in the Republican-leaning *News*, but the competing paper, the *Democrat*, was scornful in its esteem of Bridges's qualifications and character. It might have seen something the *News* and its followers didn't, but the *News* wrote in its November 9, 1889 issue:

> *The attack upon Mr. John W. Bridges, our newly appointed postmaster, at this place by the* Democrat *last week, was entirely uncalled for and out of place. Nothing in Mr. Bridges' life or conduct has ever justified such insinuations, as is cast upon him by the irresponsible cur who edits that sheet* [George W. Haskell]. *As for morals! What has the editor of the* Democrat *to boast of? His life and habits are too well known to comment upon. Mr. Bridges has held the position of operator for the Western Union Telegraph Company at this place for the past five years. He has been industrious and labored hard to support his family and get ahead in the world. He has always taken an active part in politics, and worked for his party's success. He was appointed postmaster because he had the support of nine-tenths Republicans in the county. He will make an excellent, accommodating official, and the* News *predicts that the party will have no cause to regret his appointment in the least, and the maudlin attempt of the* Democrat *to besmirch his character cannot hurt him.*

Bridges took office on October 29, 1889, and remained in that esteemed role until August 18, 1891—the day he disappeared.

It might have been the upcoming Peach Fair news or the extensive list of delinquent taxes or the fact that the circus was coming to town, but the *News* didn't note in its local section that John W. Bridges had taken a trip to Denver on August 18. Ostensibly, it was for a business trip. His prolonged absence didn't generate much curiosity—that is, until his wife and kids took off, too.

In the September 12 issue, there was much to say. By now, he'd not been seen or heard from for several weeks, but when his family left, a rumor started that maybe his post office books weren't in order. His "sureties" took possession of the post office, and one of them, W.G. Connely, was placed in charge. Immediately, a postal inspector was telegraphed for, and he arrived shortly. After going over the books, they found a shortage of $2,954.34. Just two months prior, an inspector had found the books in pristine order. His books at the Western Union office were checked, too, but were fine.

No one could say for sure that Mrs. Bridges knew what her husband was up to, but they suspected she did. And everyone was saying the man owed money heavily around town from gambling. In Denver, a friend of Bridges, B.B. Clawson, admitted he'd been lending money to Bridges for a while. He thought it a bit strange that these debts were paid back very quickly. He now knew his friend had been using post office monies to pay him back. The last loan had been for $700.

Bridges's whereabouts were a mystery to his seekers, but he had gone to Old Mexico. Mrs. Bridges moved to Denver, claiming she was unaware of her wayward husband's location. In February 1892, she filed for divorce in Mesa County, asking for custody of their four children, as well as alimony. She claimed he'd willfully deserted and abandoned her. Her divorce and custody were granted in June, since her husband didn't make an appearance. She received fifteen dollars a month for child support and another fifteen dollars for alimony until all the children were eighteen. All of which she'd get if they could find her ex-husband.

A May 23 chattel mortgage sale paid their debts, with A.D. Guild buying the elegant fixtures of the post office, which Bridges had bought with the mortgage. There was a bit of trouble picking them up, unfortunately. In July, Mr. Guild met a determined Mr. Connely, the new postmaster, who warned Guild not "to monkey with Uncle Sam's mail." The matter had to be placed in Judge Marsh's hands. The *News* doesn't state the outcome.

It finally came to light that Bridges was in Monterey, Old Mexico, but no one went after him there. In June 1892, he contacted one of his surety men, Thomas B. Crawford, and begged him, along with the other sureties, to pay his bond if he turned himself in. He promised he'd go back to Old Mexico and earn the money to pay them back.

The *News* and the townsfolk were amazed at the man's cheek. "After wronging these men so seriously he still comes to them for favors!" As far as they were concerned, he could suffer the consequences of his "folly" and repent "at leisure."

Crawford turned the letter over to the authorities, who promptly found Mr. Bridges and hauled him in. Bridges was brought to Pueblo County Jail on June 10, 1892. The *News* didn't cover this event, although it spent a lot of space thanking people for bringing a luscious box of strawberries to the *News* office and exclaiming over Mr. Waters's gorgeous gooseberry bush that "ought to go to the World's Fair."

Bridges remained in jail from June 10, 1892, to March 11, 1893—the reason why he didn't make divorce court. He was sentenced for embezzling $2,875 of the government's money. The *News* reported his sentencing on the front page. Its tone remained triumphant and judgmental. What didn't make the report was that Grand Junction businessman Ed Bouton had accompanied Bridges to court, his pockets stuffed with money donated by him and other Grand Junction businessmen who were "yet willing to believe in his possible reformation." Also missing was the news that his sympathetic lawyer spoke profusely of his good character falling prey to the "stringent" economic times in 1891.

The judge was less compassionate. He believed Bridges's acts were deliberate and sentenced him to ten months in Pueblo's county jail and to pay $2,875 plus costs.

## Adams's Sleight of Hand

The valley's quixotic tendencies to forgive its favorite sons were magnified where Orson Adams Jr. was concerned. Adams's name started cropping up in the *News* in the early 1880s. He was a Utah rancher who had holdings in Colorado. He visited Grand Junction quite often and one day decided to make it his home. In the New Year's Eve 1885 edition, the *News* wrote, "Orson Adams Jr. joins our herd this week." Within a few years, he was head cashier of Mesa County State Bank. Eventually, he became its president. He was a driving force in establishing an electric plant and the Interurban trolley, as well as the "head of the old line Republicans." He also was mayor.

It's no wonder he was involved in so many important things. He was married to Lettie Low, the daughter of Seth Low, president of Columbia University, a U.S. diplomat and mayor of New York City. As the son-in-law of such prestige, his name better be associated with fine businesses and auspicious achievements. His home, built on the southwest corner of Eleventh and Rood, was opulent, and the couple entertained frequently. He was a loving husband and doting father, even accompanying his injured daughter, Ethel, to Denver for an operation. To the public eye, he was the epitome of progressiveness.

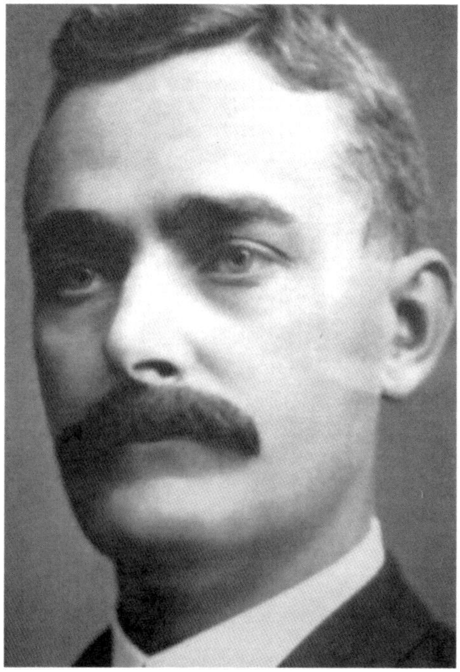

Orson Adams not only was the key promoter for the Interurban, but he was also instrumental in erecting the first steel frame edifice west of the Continental Divide. The Electric Block was located on the southwest corner of Main and Third Streets and headquartered the Grand Junction and Grand River Railway streetcar system. Through the years, it became home to the Ross Business College and the Public Service Company and even secreted offices on the second floor for World War II's Manhattan Project. *Courtesy of Loyd Files Research Library.*

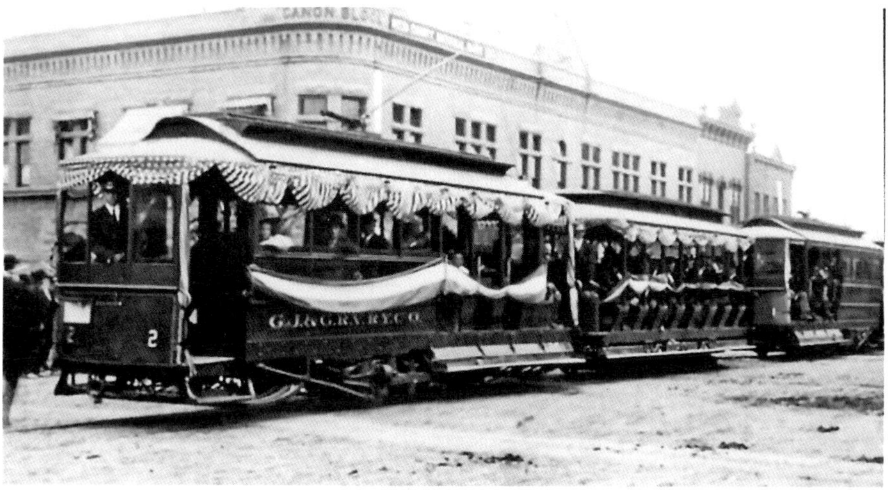

Inaugural Day for the new Interurban system was a huge celebration. Construction began on March 12, 1909, and the Last Spike ceremony took place on the afternoon of April 12 on Gunnison Avenue and Seventh Street. On May 22, the official opening drew unprecedented crowds to downtown Grand Junction. Ticket books were snatched up, and special rides were given all day. Orson Adams had become a hero to the Western Slope. *Author's collection.*

On the surface, banking in the hands of Orson Adams was good for the economy. When a silver panic hit Denver in 1893, his cheerful demeanor helped stop one from erupting in Grand Junction.

In 1910, his prosperous bank moved into the Canon Block, a magnificent building on the southwest corner of Main and Fourth. The interior was fitted up with marble counters, inlaid and highly polished hardwood floors and mahogany details, and even a cozy gas fireplace with three artificial logs warmed the directors' room.

Three years later, its doors were closed, its commander arrested for embezzling the bank's funds. Proclaiming he'd done it to save the bank, Adams had been arriving at the bank early each morning, working on a second set of financial books. A conservator was assigned to get the bank doors open again, but now Adams's cherished patrons were being paid fifty cents on every dollar.

While the bank struggled to reopen its doors, Adams pleaded guilty to forty-nine of eighty-two counts against him. Though none of the monies was used by him personally, he was convicted of misappropriation of the bank's funds and sentenced to six years in Fort Leavenworth penitentiary, beginning June 8, 1914. A model prisoner who "foiled a jail break" at Leavenworth, he was released earlier than ordered. He moved to 1550 Ogden Street in Denver and started a movie business.

When Orson Adams Jr. died in 1937, his local obituary stated that he still had many friends in Grand Junction. It praised him as the most progressive early-day citizen of the town and referred to his embezzling as a "tragic circumstance." The *Sentinel* reminded readers that the man had flaws but that his "virtues overbalanced these." The obituary concluded that Adams had accomplished great things for the young town.

## Chapter 7
# A Matter of Murder

Murder has marred the sagebrush landscape of western Colorado since the 1880s. Today's sensational murders are dissected a thousand ways by the media, but back in the olden days, death was simpler. Or was it? A 1933 headline about a boy who had a pitchfork shoved into his body or the 1910 suicide of a man who ignited two sticks of dynamite in his mouth could compete with any of today's headlines.

Murder is serious business, and yet early businesses blatantly promoted their wares with it. MURDERED capped a 1923 advertisement for the Shoeteria at 412 Main Street. It assured the public that it had "killed Mr. High Price and wanted to confess to the public that he is gone forever."

No neighborhood was untouched by murder. Highlighted in this chapter are a few of the more interesting and heart-wrenching murders that took place on the Western Slope.

## Lula Unhinged

The headline read "Orchard Mesa Woman Fatally Wounds Man." Mrs. Lula Rehkugler shot Joe Waters in the back six times on November 8, 1912, and after he "languished" at St. Mary's Hospital for a short while, he died from his wounds. This was the first murder in the area for seven years, and to have the record broken by a woman set the valley in a tizzy.

The night before the murder, Chris and Lula Rehkugler, farmers on Orchard Mesa, and their farmhand, Joseph Waters, were eating dinner when an argument broke out. Waters wanted to leave the farm, but he had wages coming to him. The Rehkuglers asked if he could wait until the proceeds from the fruit sales came in, but Waters wanted out right then. He said he'd take the workhorse and sell it for the $100 owed him. As the horse was necessary to the farm, Lula became very angry and told him she'd stop him if he tried.

The next morning, Waters was rooting around in a closet looking for his clothes. Lula had hidden them there, hoping to keep him at the farm. She pleaded with him to stay and then got angry when he continued dragging his belongings out. Storming out of the room, she returned with a recently purchased .32-caliber Smith and Wesson and emptied the bullets into the backside of Waters.

Chris heard the shots and rushed into the house. When he saw Waters on the floor, he thought he was dead and called for Sheriff Schrader, Coroner Porter and Dr. Needham. All arrived within thirty minutes, along with *Sentinel* reporter Whipple Chester. From the time they arrived, Lula acted as if this was a social call. With a pleasant voice, she invited them in and explained what had happened, as if detailing her favorite recipe.

As Lula was graciously seating her "guests," they all heard the groan. Rushing to Waters, they discovered that the wounded man was still alive. Though the doctor could see Waters was in a bad way, he dismissed the coroner and prepared the man for transfer to the hospital.

Lula continued her narrative on how her farmhand wound up on the bedroom floor with six bullets in his back. It was all about the horse, she said. In the bedroom, a different story was dispensing. The reporter, Whipple, sat down next to Waters, who was now lying on the bed, and learned that Waters and Lula were lovers and had been for a long time. Waters had wanted to leave for a while, but every time he tried, Lula would do something to keep him here. He was determined to leave this time, as he was hoping to get back with his wife. That's why Lula shot him.

Joseph Waters died at St. Mary's Hospital that evening. His autopsy was performed the night of the inquest. He had died because one of the bullets had nicked his liver, causing a fatal hemorrhage.

An inquest was held at Yunker and Callahan's "gloomy" funeral parlor on Main near Third. All the evidence involved was paraded before the coroner's jury and the suspect. Lula remained stoic while Waters's bloodied and bullet-riddled clothing was held up and through the testimonies of those involved after coming to the house. The casket that held Waters's body was near her elbow. When she finally allowed herself to look upon it, she broke down and fainted in her husband's arms.

The *Sentinel* soliloquized the scene on November 11, 1912: "Collapsing under the crushing weight of grief and remorse long pent up, Mrs. Lula Rehkugler, slayer of Joseph Waters, at last broke down this afternoon as she looked upon the pallid features of the man who said she shot him because she loved him too dearly to see him leave her." A later account would have her bending over and kissing the corpse's face.

The guilty verdict was no surprise to anyone, and Lula received the news with equanimity. She'd been held in the county jail since the day of the murder, contemplative and mostly reading her Bible. Often, she helped Mrs. Schrader with the housework around the jail. When the verdict was read, Sheriff Schrader officially arrested her.

Stating that lawyers' fees would "pauperize" her husband, Lula said she wouldn't fight the charges. Several fraternal organizations came forward and paid her lawyers.

The trial began on December 21 at the courthouse at Sixth and Main. The jury box was quickly filled, and it sensationalized the court when Lula's defense

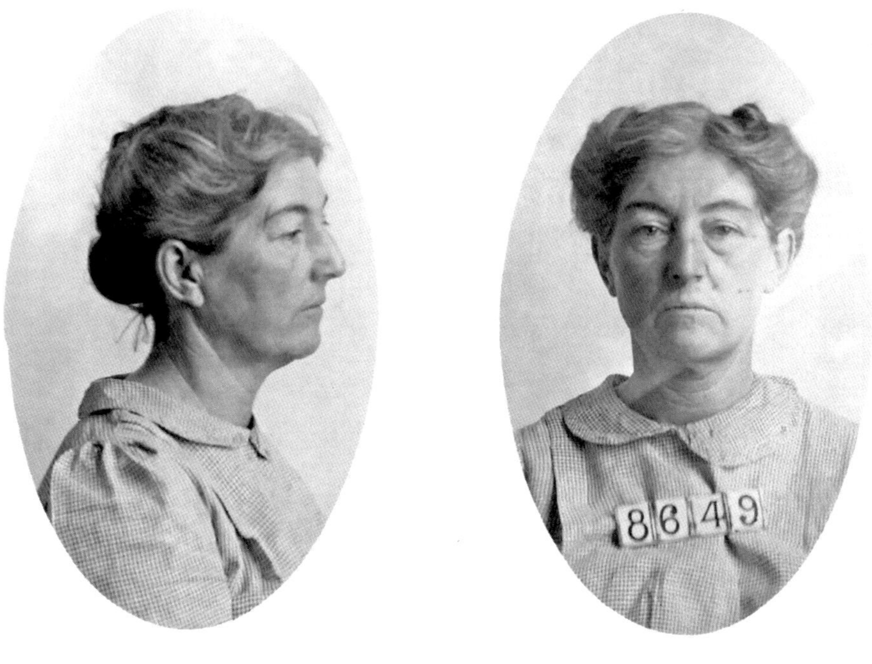


Lula Rehkugler's husband, Chris, must truly have loved his wife, for even after confessing to loving the man she killed in their home and going to prison for almost a decade, he stuck by her. They both moved to Tacoma, Washington, after her release. Lula died there in 1935, and Chris died there on October 10, 1939. *Courtesy of Colorado State Archives.*

had morphed into saying Waters was about to attack her when she shot him. She admitted to kissing the corpse but said that she didn't love him "at all."

After seeing all the evidence, the jury found Lula Rehkugler guilty of voluntary manslaughter. Her countenance remained composed, and she didn't offer a statement after the verdict was announced. The death penalty was requested and rejected. Lula became sick with the "grippe" and wasn't able to appear for her appointed sentencing. The day after New Year's 1913, Lula was finally sentenced to five to eight years of hard labor.

The news proclaimed that she was the first woman to ever commit murder in the valley, but it had forgotten about Maggie Herrick, who killed her husband's lover in 1885. But since Mr. Herrick killed Mrs. Herrick shortly thereafter, Lula would be the first woman from the Western Slope to ever enter the state penitentiary. When she was released, she and her husband, Chris, moved to Adams County and eventually to Roy, Washington, where she died in 1935.

## Shorty Jones, a Hanged Man's Chronicle

"Knights of the Road" was the romantic moniker given to tramps who hopped trains during the Depression. Walter "Shorty" Jones, Monrad Nelson, Hartford "Red" Johnson and seventeen-year-old Joe Less laughed at this. They were pragmatic, as most hobos were. They'd learned there was nothing romantic about scrounging for food and shelter every day.

October nights in the Rockies are crisp, and the four men huddled around a small fire they'd built on the floor of the freight car. The train had just passed Palisade as it headed east into De Beque Canyon along the Colorado River. Their bellies were full thanks to Red, who'd bought the boys dinner. Ex-military, he was a quiet and neat man, divorced with two children, their pictures treasured in his pocket. Red and Joe were from the East Coast, heading home to their families. Jones, who sported a leather jacket with a red "Steve" printed on its back, and Nelson were midwesterners with wandering souls.

That evening, October 18, 1932, the pragmatic sides of Jones, twenty-three, and Nelson, twenty-six, emerged. They'd noticed Red's full coin purse when he paid for their meals and had decided they wanted more than just a meal from their new friend. While the easterners sat by the fire, chuckling over some bit of humor, Jones and Nelson armed themselves with a hatchet and a heavy bolt. When the time was right, Jones split Red's skull open with the hatchet, while Nelson attacked the young boy. Less was injured but pretended to be dead in hopes that his attackers would let him be. When he heard them say, "Let's throw him out!" he struggled with them.

They hauled Red and Joe over the side of the car. Red's body hit the face of the cliff before dropping near the tracks. The boy lay where he landed with his eyes closed. The fall hadn't killed him, but he didn't want them to finish the job. Back on the train, Jones and Nelson divvied Red's money, knapsack and any other valuables and then settled by the fire and waited for a good place to disappear.

Joe watched the caboose disappear and then stumbled up. He checked on his friend. Dead. He wandered a mile or so back until he reached the McKay ranch at Palisade. It was the early morning hours, but Arthur McKay took one look at the boy's head and called the sheriff. While they waited, Joe's head wound was dressed. Joe led a posse to Red's body a mile and a half above the Palisade bridge, near the reclamation tunnel. They scoured the tracks for several miles and found what little was left of Red's belongings: his pocket book, less fifty-eight dollars, as well as the large bolt Nelson had used to hit Joe.

The authorities along the train route were asked to keep an eye out for the two derelicts. Before long, they were apprehended in Salida, the cleaned

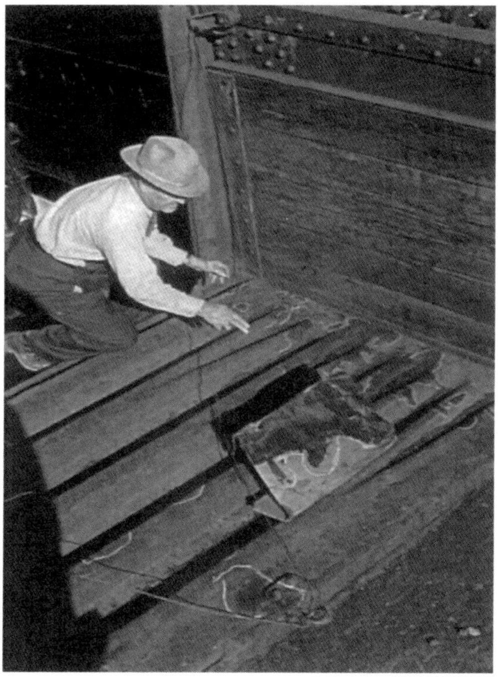

Sheriff Charles Lumley is seen here at the boxcar where the death of "Red" Johnson and assault of his young friend occurred. Lumley is pointing to a blood pool. If it weren't for the stupidity of Jones and Nelson, one wonders how long it would have taken to solve Red Johnson's murder. *Courtesy of Teri Huff.*

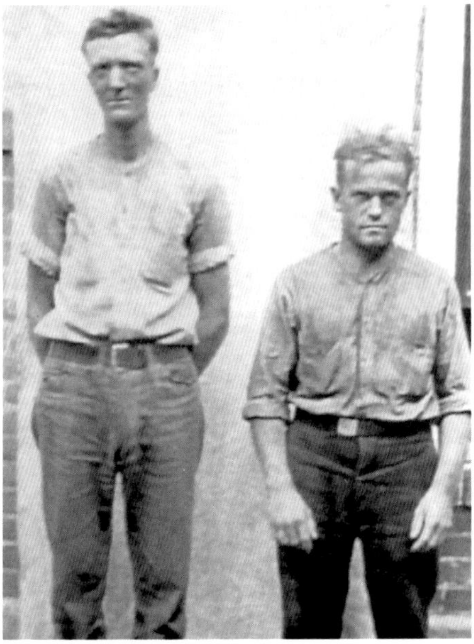

Shorty Jones and Monrad Nelson's picture at the county jail shows why Jones had his nickname. Jones met the hanging rope for his crime, but Nelson, whose victim was injured but not killed on the boxcar, went to Canon City's prison. He attempted to escape with five other prisoners in 1934. They were the night crew for the prison bakery and had managed to dig a fifty-five-foot-long tunnel before they were caught and put in solitary confinement. *Courtesy of Teri Huff.*

hatchet nestled in the knapsack Jones had stolen. Jones's rather loud jacket had given them away. Sheriff Lumley lugged them back to Grand Junction "heavily shackled."

By then, the county jail was on White Avenue, right behind the new courthouse on Rood. The two men were housed in a cell, and eventually, murder charges were filed at the courthouse. Even though they confessed to attacking the two men, a trial would determine the degree of murder. Joe Less was detained as a witness.

An autopsy took place, and Red's family was contacted. They asked that his body be buried in the Palisade cemetery. A brief, sparsely attended graveside service for the thirty-three-year-old was conducted.

The two slayers pleaded "insanity" and were sent to the Pueblo asylum for observation. Two weeks later, they were "loaded up with handcuffs and leg chains" and brought back to Grand Junction. Insanity pleas were withdrawn.

It was the shortest murder trial in local history, taking less than two days. The jury received the case late the second day and deliberated for eight and a half hours.

"Jones and Nelson Guilty of First Degree Murder" read the *Sentinel*'s December 23 headline. Jones received the death penalty and Nelson life in prison. The short man remained unmoved by the verdict. As both were

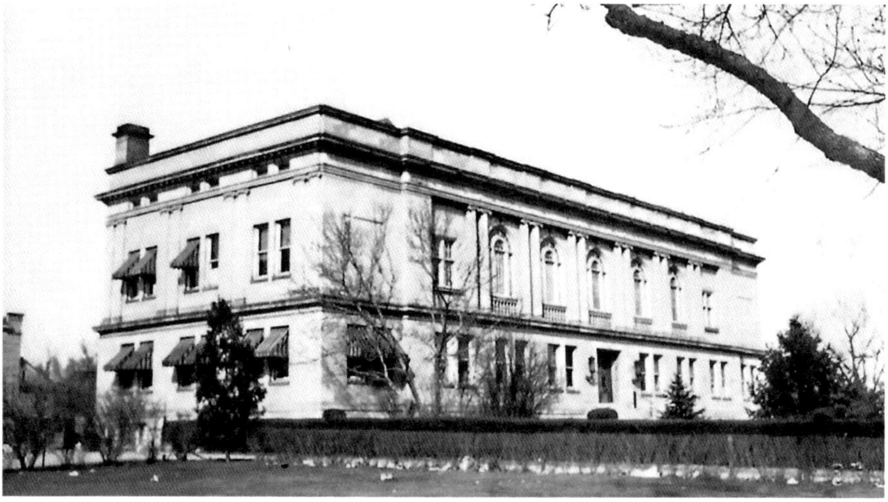

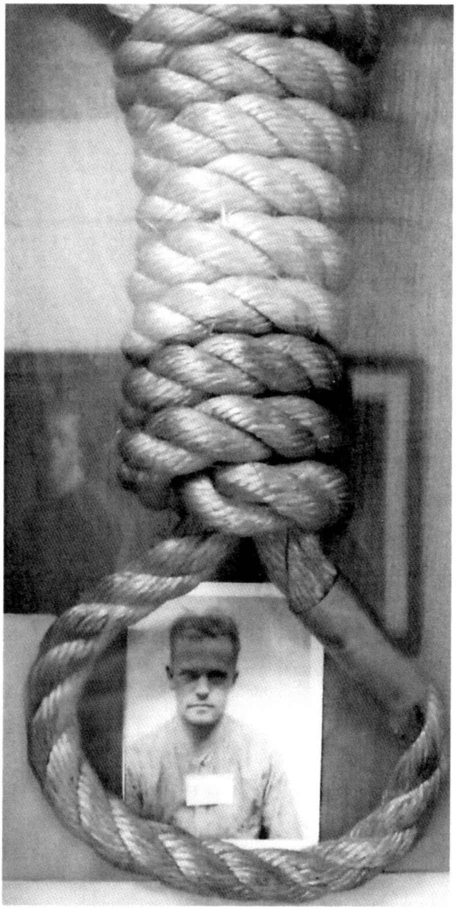

*Above*: The stately courthouse that graces the northwest corner of Rood Avenue and Sixth Street was ready for occupancy in 1925. Behind it, on White Avenue, was the third county jail. With the city jail at Sixth and Colorado, the new courthouse was perfectly placed to accommodate both sets of prisoners. Today, the courthouse is at West Main and Spruce Streets. The city and county jail are combined, as are the courts, all situated within feet of each other. *Author's collection.*

*Right*: Shorty Jones's hanging rope is on display at the Museum of Colorado Prisons in Canon City, Colorado. He was the last inmate to be "launched" into eternity via a self-spring hanging apparatus. Not only did the prisoner face his death on the gallows, but he was also responsible for setting it in motion. If the height and weight of the prisoner weren't calibrated perfectly, the prisoner could die in several gruesome ways, including having his head ripped off or taking a very long time to strangle to death. The gas chamber replaced hanging in Colorado after Shorty's extra-long demise. *Courtesy of Museum of Colorado Prisons.*

escorted out of the courthouse, Shorty Jones casually commented, "Whose nice new Ford?" as they passed a car parked outside.

Jones was the second man sentenced to death in Mesa County, the first being George McGarvey, who had escaped from county jail after hitting jailer Ed Innes over the head and killing him.

Jones appealed the decision, but the Colorado Supreme Court upheld the conviction. Just after Thanksgiving 1933, Sheriff Lumley appealed to the governor not to hang Jones. His execution was scheduled for the upcoming weekend. He hoped to get Jones's sentence commuted to life in prison. Even the *Sentinel*'s publisher, Walter Walker, wrote on behalf of Jones. The governor denied their requests.

Jones, it turns out, was the last person hanged in the Colorado penal system. He asked for a beer for his last meal and was given two. He refused the "solace of prayers" as he "nonchalantly" walked to the death house as a "blizzard howled a dirge" outside. It took fourteen minutes for the man to strangle to death, possibly because he was so small and the prison officials hadn't adjusted the settings to account for that. After his December 1, 1933 hanging, the gallows were dismantled. Jones's rope is displayed at the Colorado Prisons Museum in Canon City, Colorado.

## Charles Graham Runs Amuck

Mrs. Vina Glazier, a widow and part-time laundress, lay dead in the doorway of her 960 Third Avenue cottage. Inside, George Morris slumped on the floor, unconscious and bleeding. Blood splattered the wood walls, and pools of blood made navigation difficult for the officers who arrived on scene. In the midst of the carnage, numerous cats perched on whatever clean surface they could find, while four puppies and their momma peeked cautiously over the edge of a wooden apple box. A fire in the stove warmed the room and intensified the strong metallic odor.

The argument started early on Sunday morning, January 14, 1934. Roomer Charles Elija Graham, age forty-one, awoke and started a fire in the stove. Graham had been sleeping in his usual place on the floor near the stove. He'd covered himself with a prized blanket that belonged to Mrs. Glazier. It was her late husband's. When sparks from the fire landed on the blanket, Mrs. Glazier demanded that Graham close the stove door, but he refused. Their conversation heated up, and Graham brought another roomer, George Morris, into the argument. He accused Mrs. Glazier of having romantic feelings for the man and proclaimed he was going to throw the guy out. Mrs. Glazier said that wasn't going to happen.

Nearby, George Morris slept soundly, but Mrs. Essa Grover, owner of the cottage, awoke and emerged from her bedroom. She immediately sensed trouble and slipped outside. Running around the corner, she aroused the neighbors, Mr. and Mrs. Will Osborne, out of bed.

When she returned with the couple, her home was in a shambles and Mrs. Glazier's body was sprawled half out the door. Her broken and bleeding head rested on the porch stoop. Morris lay mortally wounded in the kitchen near the puppies' box. Graham hefted an axe and strode for the door. The frightened trio backed away. Graham stepped over Mrs. Glazier and shook the axe in their direction, asking if they wanted the same thing. They ran one way, and Graham headed the other.

The axe murderer strolled directly to the police station a few blocks away and turned himself in. Officers were dispatched to Third Avenue, and Graham was transferred to the Mesa County Jail. Sheriff Lumley took pictures and mug shots and then allowed Graham to perch on top of the steel cage to tell his story. In his hands was a deck of cards, which he played while dealing out the gruesome details of his morning. Rather than showing remorse, he

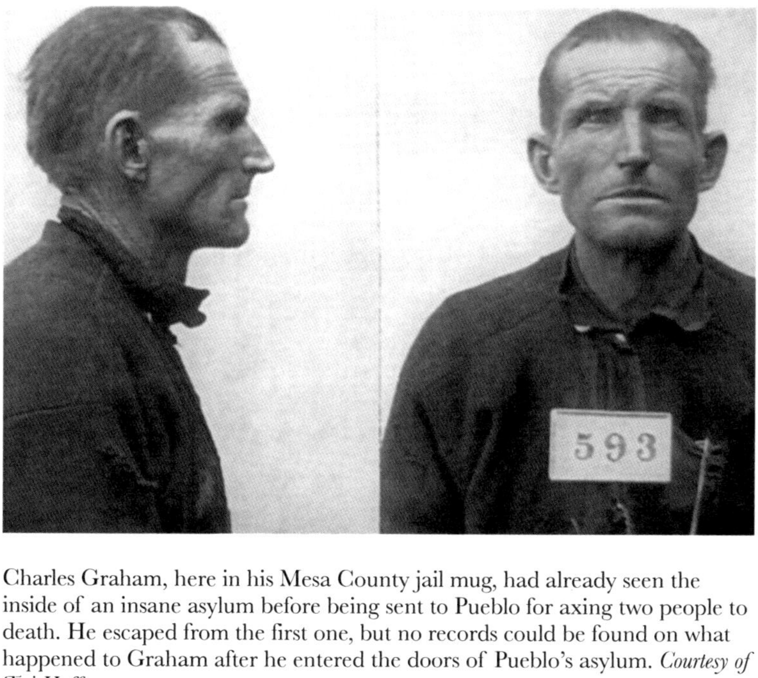


Charles Graham, here in his Mesa County jail mug, had already seen the inside of an insane asylum before being sent to Pueblo for axing two people to death. He escaped from the first one, but no records could be found on what happened to Graham after he entered the doors of Pueblo's asylum. *Courtesy of Teri Huff.*

seemed proud of his actions. He claimed Mrs. Glazier had begged him to kill her and thought he should be set free on a self-defense plea.

George Morris, who'd suffered three strikes to his head and was paralyzed on one side of his body, was rushed to St. Mary's Hospital. Little hope was offered of his recovery, and he died on January 16. Mrs. Glazier's body was autopsied and then taken to Callahan Mortuary. She was buried at Orchard Mesa Cemetery.

Graham's court-appointed attorney, William Weiser, asked that Graham be sent to Pueblo for observation. Weiser had learned that Graham had been committed in another state and had escaped. It was obvious to Weiser that the man was insane. Observed for twenty days, the asylum's Dr. Zimmerman also determined that he was insane. This was the main push for his defense at the trial.

Because the hospital wasn't within the judicial district, Dr. Zimmerman was not called to take the stand on behalf of Graham. However, the court appointed three "disinterested and capable" local doctors to examine him, one being Dr. B.L. Jefferson of the State Home for Mental Defectives. They also found Graham "dangerously insane." District Attorney William F. Haywood, however, convinced the jury that Graham was not insane, and they found him guilty of first-degree murder. Judge George W. Bruce later sentenced him to death in the gas chamber. He said he believed Graham was insane but since the jury found him guilty, he had no alternative but to sentence him to die.

Weiser appealed to the Supreme Court, without success.

Graham's case caught the eye of Denver lawyer Gail Ireland. The "Champion of the Underdog" had decided to stump for Graham. He believed the man was insane and shouldn't die because of that. Stating, "The verdict is incomprehensible," he called for a retrial. The day before Graham was supposed to die in the gas chamber, a stay of execution was ordered, and he was remanded back to district court for a new trial.

The second trial took place in Grand Junction in December 1934. Unlike what had happened at his spring trial, Graham took the stand this time. The *Sentinel* reported on December 18, 1934: "Clasping his worn Bible tightly, his small black eyes glittering, the defendant, interspersed his anwers [*sic*] to attorneys' questions with numerous brief discourses on religion. So rapidly did the words tumble from his mouth that he occasionally became incoherent, necessitating repetitions of his remarks."

Graham went on to say that God had told him to kill Mrs. Glazier. He said it wasn't against the law to kill if God told him to. The jury found him guilty by reason of insanity, and he was sent to the Pueblo insane asylum.

## Joe Arridy, Innocent at Last!

Gail Ireland's influence figured greatly in another convicted killer's story. Joe Arridy was executed in 1937, and his death has touched many lives since. His saga began when he escaped from the Colorado State Home and Training School for Mental Defectives, located just outside Grand Junction's city limits.

Joe, of Syrian descent, was the only child of Henry and Mary Arridy. He had the mental capacity of a six-year-old. Born in 1915, he'd lived at the Home since the age of eleven. On August 9, 1936, he, along with three buddies, escaped and hopped a train for Pueblo, where Joe had once lived. All four wound up back in Grand Junction, but when his three friends turned themselves in, Joe held back. He wasn't quite ready to give up the adventure.

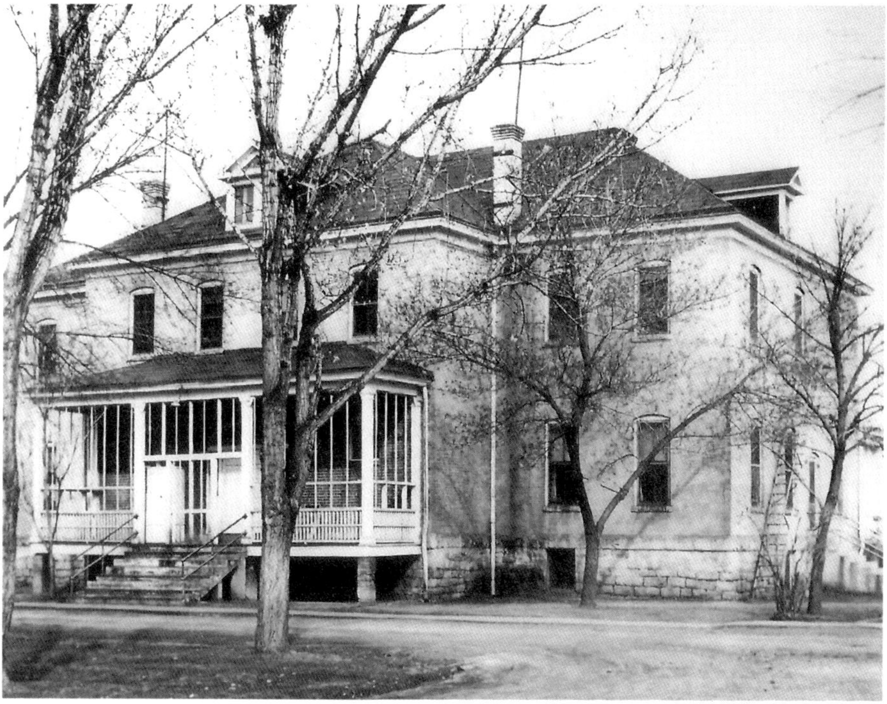

The State Home still exists outside Grand Junction's city limits. It is purported to be haunted due to the nature of its inmates' mental and emotional capacities, as well as reported abuses at one time or another. Despite the occasional infractions and punishment of the perpetrators, many former employees loved working there and retired with fond memories. *Courtesy of Loyd Files Research Library.*

Back on the train he went, and a few days later, he landed at the railroad yards in Cheyenne, Wyoming. Joe offered to work for food at the railroad kitchen and became a dishwasher. When the company pulled up stakes and moved, Joe was left behind. He was arrested for vagrancy and turned over to the Laramie County Sheriff's Office. His arrest became the cornerstone of a bizarre house of cards that toppled on Arridy.

A brutal hammer slaying had occurred in Pueblo on August 2, 1936. Sally Crumply, seventy-two, and Mrs. R.O. McMurtree, forty-eight, were bludgeoned on the head while asleep. Crumply died from her wounds, while McMurtree survived. Two weeks later, and three blocks away, two sisters, Dorothy Drain, fifteen, and Barbara Drain, twelve, were attacked in the same way. Dorothy died, and Barbara survived. The city, understandably, was in a panic and wanted someone arrested. The attacker was identified by Mrs. McMurtree, and Frank Aguilar, a Mexican national, was arrested. That should have been the end of it.

Enter Laramie County sheriff George J. Carroll. Carroll was famous for breaking up Ma Barker's gang and had assisted in rescuing the Boettcher family's kidnapped child. He liked the limelight. After he arrested Arridy for vagrancy, he found out that Joe was from Pueblo. Remembering the attacks there, he thought maybe he'd caught the killer. With a little prompting, he got Joe to admit to the killings, even though Joe had still been at the State Home when the first attack occurred. Carroll contacted Pueblo Police chief J. Arthur Grady and said he had the murderer.

This surprised Grady, but they hadn't gotten a confession from Aguilar yet. He was presented with a quandary. They had plenty of evidence on Aguilar but no confession. They had no evidence on Arridy but a confession, even if it had changed numerous times. His mind was made up when a witness placed Arridy in Pueblo at the time of Dorothy Drain's attack.

Aguilar finally admitted to the four attacks and decided to include Joe in the confession. He claimed they'd committed the crimes together and then split up.

Both men went to trial, and Joe's attorney entered a plea of not guilty by reason of insanity. He was examined and found incapable of distinguishing right from wrong. And yet a jury found him legally sane. During his April 1937 trial, he was his usual sweet self. But a desire to please led him to give answers that incriminated him, and he was found guilty.

On August 13, 1937, Frank Aguilar was executed without changing his story.

Joe Arridy was sent to the penitentiary at Canon City under Warden Roy Best. Best liked Joe and understood his mental capacity. He felt bad for the

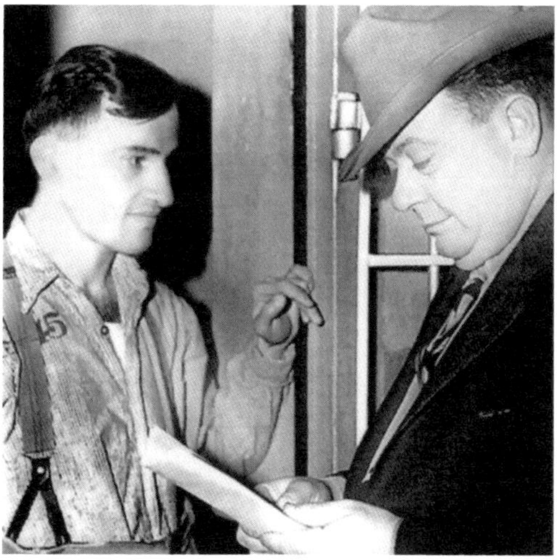

Joseph Arridy, seen here with Warden Roy Best, was like a beloved son to Best. He gave Joe a toy train one time, and before Joe walked to the gas chamber, he gave it to one of his fellow inmates. Best worked tirelessly to get Joe's death sentence commuted, as did others. Joe's death left a hollow in many hearts that changed the way the mentally disabled are treated in the corrections system. *Courtesy of Colorado Museum of Prisons.*

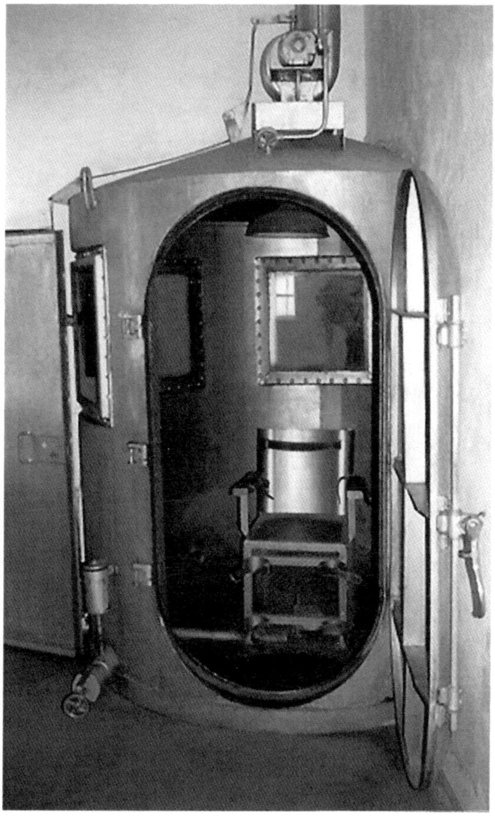

Canon City's gas chamber is now on display at the Colorado Museum of Prisons. Warden Best helped design it and was pleased that it was much quicker and more humane than the gallows before it. Among its victims was John Gilbert Graham, who planted twenty-five sticks of dynamite in his mother's suitcase before she got on an American Airlines plane in Denver on the evening of November 1, 1955. It exploded and killed his mother and forty-three other travelers. He died in the gas chamber on January 11, 1957. *Courtesy of Colorado Museum of Prisons.*

boy and treated him like a son. He gave Joe toys to play with and even brought him home to celebrate Christmas with his family.

For nearly two years, appeals were pursued on behalf of Joe. Gail Ireland fought tirelessly for him to commute the death sentence. On the day of his execution by asphyxiation, Joe gave his toy train to a fellow prisoner. He asked for ice cream as his last meal and went to the gas chamber with a happy smile on his face. Roy Best wrote a heart-wrenching poem about his love and sadness for Joe.

Through the efforts of Gail Ireland, author Robert Perske, Friends of Joe Arridy, attorney David Martinez and many others, Joe Arridy was granted a full and unconditional pardon by Colorado governor Bill Ritter on January 7, 2011. The press release stated:

> *An overwhelming body of evidence indicates that 23-year-old Arridy was innocent, including false and coerced confessions, the likelihood that Arridy was not in Pueblo at the time of the killing, and an admission of guilt by someone else…Granting a posthumous pardon is an extraordinary remedy. But the tragic conviction of Mr. Arridy and his subsequent execution on Jan. 6, 1939, merit such relief based on the great likelihood that Mr. Arridy was, in fact, innocent of the crime for which he was executed, and his severe mental disability at the time of his trial and execution. Pardoning Mr. Arridy cannot undo this tragic event in Colorado history. It is in the interests of justice and simple decency, however, to restore his good name.*

## BIG KID EAMES ROLLS SNAKE EYES

The Depression separated the wheat from the chaff, so to speak. For the most part, people tried to stay positive. Citizens helped out one another, and parents used the strained circumstances to build character in their children. Carefully tended gardens and fruit of the farm animals not only satisfied the family's diet, but there were usually leftovers to feed a hobo or two as well.

The Depression also dredged up the seedier side of society. Mug shots of the era framed desperate eyes, disheveled hair and rumpled and dirty clothes. Some who peered back at the jail camera were simply desperate family men turned temporary criminals out of need. A lot of them were simply opportunists.

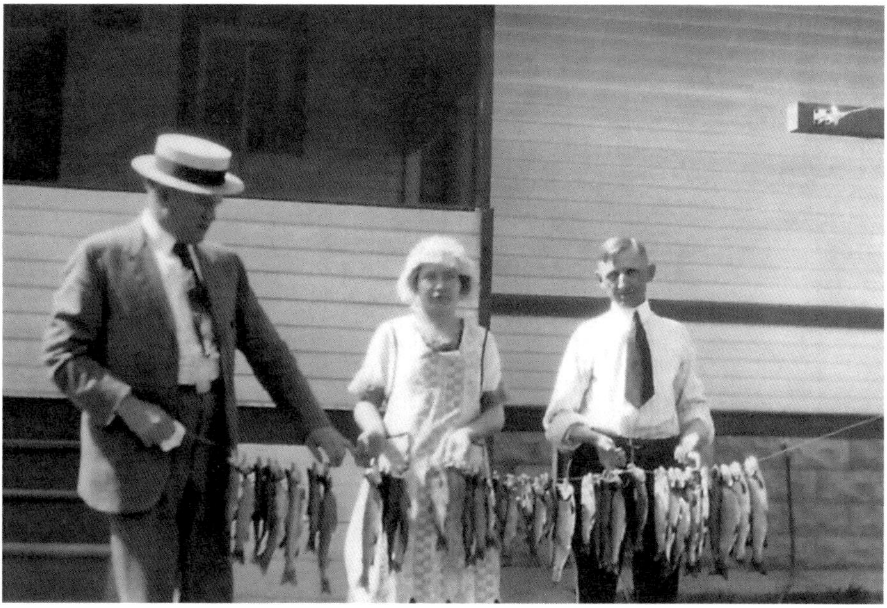

Regarding Big Kid Eames, a story persists even today about his funeral. Some people remember that it took place in the Avalon Theater on Main at Seventh. Further details recount the front row seating all the fancy prostitutes in the city who'd come to pay their respects. The newspaper has a different story. It relays the information that it took place at Martin's Funeral Home on Colorado, right behind the Avalon Theater. No mention of prostitutes is included in the article. That's not to say he wasn't a friend. *Courtesy of Loyd Files Research Library.*

The Western Slope had its share of no-goods. Lying on the railroad routes, the town was inundated with hobos, petty thieves and confidence men. There was the occasional murderer, too.

At the time, gambling ran rampant, especially in Grand Junction. By the mid- to late 1930s, several murders had shocked the town. Jeanette Morris was strangled to death in the red-light district, the Barbary Coast. There'd been a shootout and murder on crowded Main Street that had ties to gambling. And then Walter "Big Kid" Eames was shot and killed.

Not that the trio of crooks had set out to murder the man who ran the Biltmore Club. Lodged above the JCPenney department store and the Golden Pheasant Café, at the northwest corner of Main and Fourth Streets, the Biltmore hid gambling tables behind a guarded door.

Eames was well known in town and well thought of, even though everyone knew his business. He was a generous and honest man and donated heavily to worthy causes. As a matter of fact, the day he was killed, two hundred

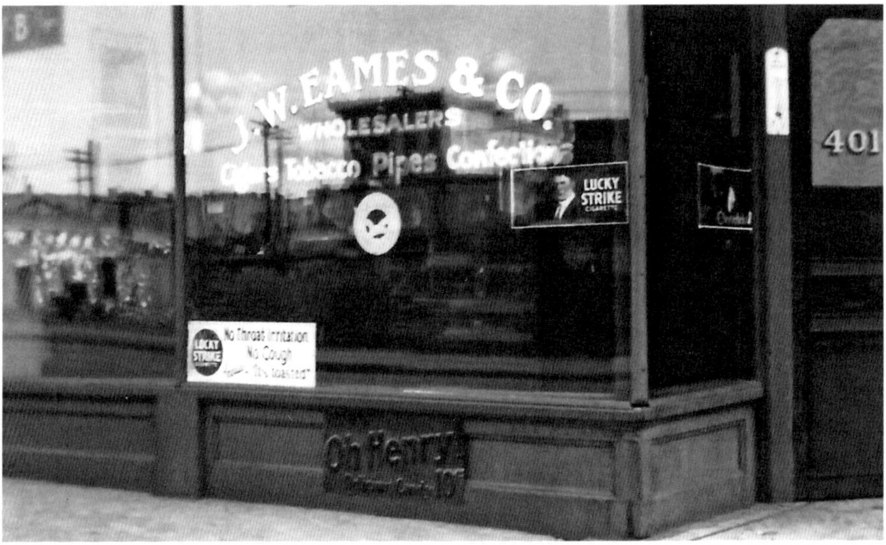


J. Walter Eames was a cigar and tobacco wholesaler in the early 1920s. His store was at 401 Colorado Avenue, which no longer exists. In the 1930s, he opened the Biltmore Club in the upper floor of the Reed Building. JCPenney had long been a tenant on the ground floor. The Biltmore had a dumbwaiter to the Golden Pheasant Café, where Eames sent midnight orders. *Courtesy of Loyd Files Research Library.*

personally prepared Christmas baskets awaited pickup at his home at 726 Chipeta. They would be distributed to the poor.

Around midnight on December 18, 1938, Eames was collecting dinner orders for his patrons. He did this every night at no charge. He sent the list down to the Golden Pheasant Café beneath the Biltmore. About the same time, three masked robbers forced their way into the crowded gambling rooms. One held a sawed-off shotgun, rather haphazardly. Witnesses said they all seemed nervous. Eames didn't hesitate to accommodate their demands.

With the flick of a nervous finger, everyone's lives changed, especially Eames's. Shotgun Man found himself holding a smoking gun and staring at a man with half a face. He hadn't meant to shoot Eames, and now he didn't know what to do about it. His buddies dragged him out the back door, and then everyone in the room descended on Eames to see if he could be saved. He was taken to the hospital, where he died an hour later.

At the inquest, a witness stated he recognized the voice of one of the men, and soon forty-year-old Fern Sadler, a parolee from San Quentin, was arrested. He and his mother ran a local dance hall, the Mile-a-Way. Police Chief Hardy Decker, Sheriff Charley Lumley and Denver investigator Walter Byron worked together to find the other two men. In February, a break came in the case, and the last two men were arrested. One confessed, and then the others followed.

Fern "Bubbles" Sadler was the brains of the robbery scheme. The trigger-happy shooter was Otis Slane, and safecracker John "Tommy" Homutoff never got to use his talents that night. Tommy was a strange-looking man. He had lost his nose while trying to blow up a safe with nitroglycerin. The flying safe door had sheared his nose right off. The prison doctor did what he thought was best for the situation. He grafted Homutoff's left little finger to the nose area, with it still attached to his hand. It took six weeks for the graft to take, and then it was cut off the hand. Homutoff went to San Quentin for the safe-blowing gig. He made friends with Sadler and Slane there.

Upon investigating, it was found that this ring of crooks had hit several states. Sadler even confessed that they had set a competing dance hall on fire the summer before.

According to an oral history of retired cop Fritz Becker, all three men stayed under the radar after they were paroled. Sadler moved back to Grand Junction, where he led a quiet life. He owned the popular Snow Peak Drive In and died in 1966. Becker ran into Homutoff on a Denver street and learned that he was down on his luck, and Slane moved to Salida to be near his sister.

With Eames's murder solved and the onset of World War II, crime settled down for a while on the Western Slope.

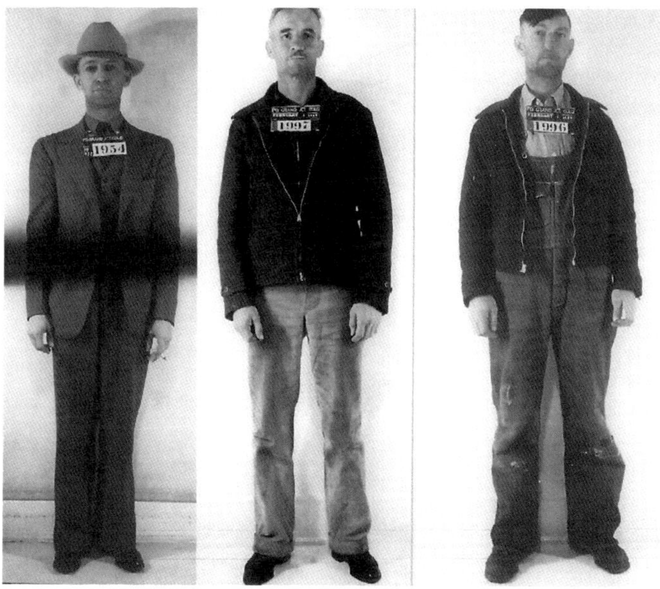


Fern Sadler, Otis Slane and John Homutoff were fellow inmates at San Quentin and got together after their release to plan the robbery of the Biltmore Club. They swear they hadn't meant to kill Eames, whom Sadler liked. After their stints in prison, they all went legit, as far as public record reveals. *Courtesy of Teri Huff.*

## HE BOUGHT THE FARM

"Wild With Excitement" was the headline of the *News*' March 24, 1900 advertisement. The "Wonder Worker," Dr. William DeCaux Tilney, appeared at the Park Opera House. His mixture of "gentle medicines" and osteopathy—a new medical procedure at the time—wowed the large audience.

Akin to the religious tent revivals making the rounds at the turn of the century, Dr. Tilney brought up the crippled, the blind and the chronically ill and cured them. Hallelujahs and broken crutches scattered across the stage, attesting to the doctor's moniker.

It's no "wonder" the doctor was so successful. The local newspaper in 1900 had several obituaries each issue. People were dying a lot. And lots of medical advertisements preyed on the suffering. Chamberlain's Pain Balm, Dr. Pierce's Golden Medical Discovery and Parker's Hair Balsam were top sellers. Cascarets Candy Cathartic helped "anything from headache to cancer and will put your bowels right," and Dr. Pierce's Pleasant Pellets cured biliousness. One woman was cured of infertility after taking three bottles of Dr. Pierce's Favorite Prescription, two bottles of Golden Medical Discovery and "some" of the Pleasant Pellets. She now had a "bright little boy."

Dr. Tilney, born in England but naturalized in the United States, was an actual doctor, having graduated from Indiana Eclectic College and studied medicine at Louisville Medical Institute. He lived in Indiana and traveled around the country, claiming his cures treated everything from "Big Neck, bladder and kidney diseases, bowel complaint, debility, dropsy, heart, liver and nerve disease, rheumatism, scrofula, loss of manly vigor, all female disorders, tape worm, sore legs, all eye and ear diseases, cancers, piles and fistula." Furthermore, they "cured without cutting or pain."

He had testimonies to back up his claims. Trinidad, Colorado bookkeeper E.M. Strait wrote this five days after his miracle, and it appeared in the *Weekly Argus News* on September 15, 1900:

> *I hereby assert that the treatment received by me for rheumatism in the opera house from Dr. Tilney, February 5, 1900, when my crutches were broken, has been a complete success and I continue to improve in strength daily. I am entirely free from pain or stiffness. Whereas I could not sleep half the night for pain, I now sleep soundly all night and can and have walked every day since without aid. I am 61 years old and well known.*

Grand Junction's appearance was summarized by the *News* in eloquent language. Dr. Tilney and "his man," Jeffers, were "agreeable and forceful speakers" and had the audience on the edge of their seats as they listened to the theories behind "their wonderful discoveries." Promises of amazing healing flowed, astounding the audience when the hard of hearing were brought up and administered to. All of a sudden, they could hear a pin drop! That was nothing compared to what happened next:

> *The doctors then called for cripples, and A.E. Pelton was brought forward on a chair by four men. He had been suffering four years with rheumatism and for the past three weeks in bed, not even able to go at times on crutches. Mr. Pelton is foreman of the* Star *office. He was operated on for twenty minutes with medicine and walked off home free from pain and stiffness, followed by the wondering crowd, while the doctor broke his crutches. To say the vast audience was astonished and wild would be putting it mildly. The doctors were warmly congratulated. It seemed like a dream, but it is real. Ministers and doctors were in the audience and seemed as well pleased as any.*

Plenty of the doctor's cures were snatched up after the demonstration, but the next day, they were being dumped in outhouses. The death of Ed Skinner prompted this. The next week's newspaper reported that Skinner, a laborer who'd just bought a farm in Whitewater, had watched the doctor perform his magic and purchased some of his potions. He paid a sum of over sixty dollars and then went home to experience the healing he was sure to get. Instead, he got worse and worse until "death occurred" before a doctor could reach him.

Drs. Tilney and Jeffers were arrested and charged with murder. They proclaimed there was nothing in the medicines that could harm anyone "in the least." A hearing took place and then adjourned to await the analysis of the medicine.

Nothing was mentioned in the following papers, so it is assumed they found nothing dangerous in the doctor's concoctions and the men were set free. Was it a matter of murder? We will never know.

Dr. Tilney returned to Indiana and died in 1925, a "venerable doctor who acquired fame years ago." He died of apoplexy.

*Chapter 8*

# Backtracks

When the Rio Grande Railway finally completed its way to Grand Junction, it was truly a day to celebrate. November 22, 1882's event "united us by two steel rails with all parts of the United States."

At 4:50 p.m., the Sierre la Sal, Engine No. 83, eased over the railroad bridge—finished one hour prior—and into the town of Grand Junction. The passengers were townsfolk who'd walked over the bridge and boarded the train on the south side of the Grand River. The *News* waxed eloquent on what this would mean for the future of the Western Slope: prosperous farms, growing towns and cities and immense factories and businesses. Today, all that and much more has transpired here.

Trains have been a mixed blessing, mostly good. They are considered a romantic addition to the country's landscape, steaming across rolling country hills or through steel and glass city jungles. They carry everything essential to the clockwork of the working masses and, in times past, provided luxurious travel.

Some visitors to Grand Junction's Union Depot have been famous. Presidents have spoken from the back of beautifully appointed Pullmans, and celebrities like Helen Keller and her teacher, Annie Sullivan; pugilist Jack Dempsey (who also lived in Grand Junction for a time); and Civil War general William Tecumseh Sherman made stops at the height of their fame.

However, along with passengers and payload, pain and death have added their own boxcar to that long, somewhat mournful queue.

## Calamity Train

Although the worst train wreck in Colorado's history took place west of Dotsero, its ties to Grand Junction are immense. The conductor responsible for this calamity was Gus Olsen, who lived in Grand Junction. A time discrepancy was the cause.

Olsen was the engineer for Denver & Rio Grande No. 5 passenger train heading west from Denver. He'd been ordered to wait at Dotsero's siding to allow another train to pass, and he was almost there. No. 5 skimmed past snowy ground that dimly glowed under the last quarter moon. Perhaps the low light contributed to him reading his watch wrong—9:45 p.m. instead of 9:50 p.m.—but he thought he could reach the siding outside Dotsero before the oncoming eastbound freight train needed the rail. His brother, Sig, was conducting that train.

He opened his throttle fully, getting the train up to forty-five miles per hour, an easy task as they were on a downhill grade. Within moments, the passenger and freight train collided in the darkness, causing the most deadly train crash Colorado has ever suffered. The *Daily Sentinel* reported on January 16, 1909, "The three monster engines telescoped with the impact, and when they came to a standstill they resembled one huge piece of twisted iron and steel."

The *Carbon County News* wrote: "In an instant all was chaos and confusion, the cries of the maimed and dying mingling with the hiss and roar of escaping steam, while over all hovered the blackness of midnight, broken only by a tongue of flame here and there as the fire fiend took possession of the wreck."

Also crushed beyond recognition were the baggage, express, smoker and day coaches, as well as three of the Pullmans. An eyewitness later said that the diner was not wrecked, but the dishes and furniture were smashed and "tossed about." Mattresses were brought in to the diner and the injured laid upon them. One passenger, a young doctor, took charge. He, joined by two women, tore sheets and pillowcases into bandages, triaged the wounded and administered morphine. Soon the anguished cries softened.

Many of the passengers had been beheaded, and mangled bodies made it difficult to identify them. Quite a few of the dead and injured were from Grand Junction and nearby towns. Bodies and wreckage were strewn around the midnight landscape. The sight was horrific. A fire broke out, and uninjured passengers used boards to shovel snow onto the flames. They also heroically tried to extricate passengers who were pinioned beneath the

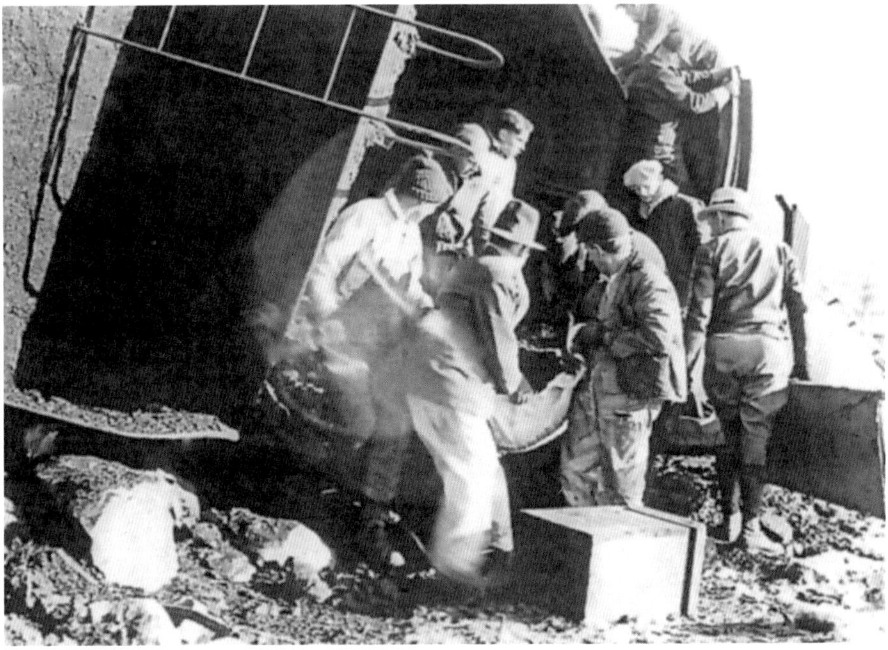

Train wrecks on the Western Slope were almost an everyday occurrence. There seemed to be broken bridges and bouncing boulders everywhere. Rockslides along De Beque Canyon stopped trains in their tracks, usually with someone getting hurt. Deaths, maiming and late trains were the norm in the early years. *Courtesy of Teri Huff.*

wreckage. When morning came, "a heavy frost and fog was over everything," according to the *Nebraska State Journal* of January 28, 1909.

Sig Olsen, the conductor of the freight train, had been pinned under the wreckage, according to Willa Soncarty, registrar of the Glenwood Springs Frontier Historical Society and Museum, in a February 6, 2006 *Post Independent* article. "Snow along the tracks was the only thing saving him from being scalded by the engine's hot water. Fireman John Anderson rescued Olsen from the debris."

Another engineer, William Jeffreys, didn't make it.

A relief train, full of doctors and nurses from Glenwood Springs, made its way to the site and carried the injured to the Glenwood depot for transport to the hospital.

At first it was thought Gus Olsen had died in the crash. A later report said he was suffering from serious internal injuries and was at the Glenwood Springs hospital. The *Sentinel* reported that his wife left from Grand Junction to be with her husband. It wrote, "Mr. Olsen is one of the best known railroad men and citizens of Grand Junction." The whole town was "stunned," but citizens offered "expressions of sympathy" to Gus Olsen and his family.

People "thronged" the newspaper and railroad offices for updates. Anxious family members awaited news of their loved ones. The *Sentinel* was inundated with Associated Press information, mostly accurate, but sought out information on its own, too.

Amazing stories began piling up and eventually made headlines. Mrs. Frank P. Robinson, whose engineer husband had died in Salida, was returning to Grand Junction with their children and his remains. Mrs. Robinson and her children were all safe and uninjured, but the body of Mr. Robinson couldn't be found. One little girl, Alice, was found alive, crunched underneath her mother's dead body. She was originally thought to be dead because she was covered in her mother's blood.

The next day, the tracks had been cleared, debris having been thrown to the side of the tracks so traffic could resume. A second search through the wreckage ensued, checking for bodies and any injured. Details of the crash unfolded.

As the days passed, the death toll rose. There were 136 passengers on the No. 5, and most were accounted for. The *Nebraska State Journal*'s March 19 issue listed the dead. Among them was "the tramp crushed between the engine and baggage car." In all, 26 people lost their lives, and 33 were injured.

Gus Olsen gave up conducting soon afterward and took up ranching. He was fondly remembered in his obituary.

## Hold That Train!

It was the end of summer in 1915. Hobos were so plentiful that "hobo hotels" were cropping up all over the country. Interest in these enterprises brought to town Jack Retlaw, who founded the first one in Seattle. The first night he opened his hotel, 676 men showed up. He was also a cartoonist, and while in town, he was going to present an entertaining program using his drawing skills at the Lyceum Theater on Main Street on the night of August 10.

The same day Retlaw came into town on the train, a young hobo, no older than twenty, died. While riding on No. 19 that morning, he'd been "scalped" as he clung to the top of a Pullman car. He held on until the train pulled into Union Depot, and then he dropped to the tracks. His head was crushed. A doctor was called, but little could be done for him.

It was believed that the young man, whose pockets revealed no identity, had stuck his head up just as the train went through the train tunnel east of Palisade (the Beaver Tail Tunnel) and smacked his head against the structure. Nothing is said about his burial, and it's possible he was interred at Potter's Field.

## Disconnected Deer

Some experiences need to be told with their original voices. Here's a January 23, 1886 *Grand Junction News* train story told by the editor. He and C.N. Cox were returning from Grand Junction after serving on jury duty:

> *We took the train for Whitewater* [southeast of Grand Junction] *at about eight o'clock a.m. and had gone only about three miles when we heard the whistle of "down brakes," and some one yelled: "Where is your gun?" I rushed to the door and saw some deer running to the left up the bluff. Mr. Cox also jumped the car, just as some one said: "Look to the right." I looked and saw a large buck and doe. The train had split a band in two. One part took to the bluffs, but the two had got caught and made for the river on the ice. The ice was very smooth and down they went, lying perfectly helpless, right opposite the caboose. Cox was equal to the occasion. Taking a lariat which I happened to have, we quickly secured the buck and others on the train secured the doe. The buck was placed on the front of the cab and the doe on the engine and away we went. When we got to Whitewater, I discovered the unfortunate buck had lost his head and horns, I suppose for the benefit of the conductor, and we dumped the body off for the benefit of the neighbors.*

## Stopped in Their Tracks

Train robberies weren't prevalent on the Western Slope, though it was a favorite pastime for ruffians elsewhere. There was that one time, in June 1907, when Kid Curry, aka Harvey Logan, a member of Butch Cassidy's Hole in the Wall Gang, boarded a Denver & Rio Grande Railroad westbound train outside of Grand Valley (Parachute). He and two other gang members blew up the safe, hoping to find gold, and then took off for Battlement Mesa. After a lively chase, Kid Curry committed suicide. The other two, as well as any booty they got, disappeared.

Then there was the Salt Lake train that headed westward from the Grand Junction depot, only to be stopped in its tracks shortly before Whitewater. As he approached Unaweep landing, the engineer noticed a pile of debris on the track and halted the train to investigate. According to the *Grand Junction News* of November 5, 1887, "No sooner had the engine came to a standstill, than the engineer and fireman were covered with rifle and firearms and commanded to dismount, and hold their hands above their heads, which they did, and were kept in this position during the entire halt."

The conductor and brakeman ran forward to see what was going on, and they, too, were ordered to get their hands up. The robbers entered the mail car and milled through the mail, not garnering much in the search. Then they headed to the express car but couldn't get in. By now, the express man knew the train was being robbed and had barricaded the doors. He "warned the robbers he was prepared for war."

Even though the express man could not have gotten inside the locked safe, the robbers persisted for fifty minutes. They finally gave up and let the train go. It arrived at 2:00 a.m. in Whitewater, where officials were notified. The robbers headed for the Gunnison River and jumped into a boat. They paddled toward Utah.

Nine men formed a posse and went toward the river, thinking they had hidden horses, but by then they had escaped. A reward of $3,000 was set by the railroad. Sheriff Bradish and his deputies continued to search, but without success.

The *Aspen Times* reported more details on December 17:

> *In the early part of November an east-bound Rio Grande express was held up…finally one of the detectives stumbled on to an old camp of robbers and there picked up a scrap of paper. This paper contained an Aspen address on it. He at once came to this point to unravel the mystery of who had the paper and how it came into their possession. He was finally convinced that two men who had made Aspen their headquarters for a short time were the parties who dropped the paper, and obtaining a minute description of the men gave chase. He went to the place they were supposed to have gone to after leaving Aspen, and found they had left that point about the right time to have reached Grand Junction. He next got wind of them on Rock Creek (southwest of Pueblo) and chased all over that section without meeting his quarry, and finally sight has been lost of the whole outfit. It is now confidently believed the train robbers will soon be brought back to answer the charge.*

One wonders where they get that confidence.

On the last day of 1887, two men were arrested in Vernal, Utah, but the local papers doubted they were the guilty ones, as they were well known in the area. Gunnison County sheriff Doc Shores arrested Ira (aka Bob) and Jack Smith and Ed Rhodes and took them to Gunnison for "safe keeping."

In January 1888, they were taken to Denver for trial in U.S. Court. The fourth robber, named Boyle, was captured finally and joined them. In July, Rhodes and Boyle pleaded guilty and were sentenced to five years at Wyoming Penitentiary. Ira and Jack Smith pleaded not guilty. Their trial was set for the next term of court.

That wasn't the end of the story. In 1886, a sensational trial kept the Western Slope on the edge of their buckboards. John L. Campbell had been accused of murdering Samuel Jones.

The gist of the case was painstakingly laid out by the *News* on July 18, 1891:

> *Jones and Campbell were interested in ranching and cattle growing in what is known as the Unaweep region, about twenty miles distant from Grand Junction. Campbell was the active manager for the firm and remained steadily on the ranch or rode the range as necessity required, caring for their stock. Jones had mining interests at Silverton and spent most of his time in the vicinity of that place. In the summer of 1886, he thought the time opportune to pay a visit to the Unaweep ranch to see how matters were shaping and counsel with Campbell as to the advisement of increasing the herds and making other improvements. After a stay of several days at the picturesque home-ranch in the beautiful canon of the Unaweep, the unfortunate Jones left the cabin in the afternoon of May 19th, 1885, for Silverton and was never thereafter seen alive.*

Campbell left that same day, heading for the summer range, and two days later returned with Jones's horse but no Jones. Two months passed before someone realized Jones hadn't been seen for a while. A large manhunt, including Campbell, set out to look for him. They found his body "at the base of a huge perpendicular cliff near the summer range." He'd been shot. Near the body was a watch chain that matched Campbell's. The man also carried a .44-caliber gun, the same size bullets in Jones.

At the trial, prosecution believed Campbell wanted all of the property, and since he and Jones were equal partners, it all now belonged to Campbell. Also, the physical evidence, though circumstantial, was very strong: bloody blankets found at the summer range cabin, the bullets, the watch chain, etc.

Twenty-three-year-old Campbell was convicted of second-degree murder and sentenced to thirty-three years behind bars.

Enter Ira and Jack Smith. Living in Unaweep territory, they had been intensely interested in the court proceedings. They had, in fact, been vocal witnesses and "fairly boiled over with zeal in their efforts to fasten the crime on Campbell." Ira was not happy with the lighter conviction and swore he would kill Campbell when he stepped out of the courtroom. The brothers organized a lynch mob, and Sheriff Cramer moved the prisoner to secret quarters. The mob gave him a "tongue-lashing." Campbell was transferred to prison and was still there when astounding news came to light.

While awaiting their trials in Denver, Jack and Ira Smith met Newt Vorce, "the terror of Deer Trail." He had the "playful habit of shooting holes through people he didn't fancy." While the trio exchanged war stories, Vorce learned something he hoped would benefit him someday. After their trials, the Smiths were sent to Laramie, Wyoming, to serve their prison terms, and Vorce went to Canon City.

Before they parted, Vorce was approached by his new friend, Ira Smith, and given a letter. Smith asked that it be brought to a man named McGill, and it contained a map of where Sam Jones's bridle, saddle, revolver and $1,600 were buried. The "treasure" was located "not over 300 yards from the shanty at the summer ranch." Smith said he'd "bought a new brace of revolvers for the purpose of shooting Campbell in case he squealed on him." Vorce believed that Ira Smith, and not "Johnny" Campbell, was the one who killed Sam Jones, though Smith didn't openly confess. Campbell's council was ecstatic.

After some sleuthing, the spot was found, causing "large and benevolent smiles." However, none of the items was buried there. Also, it was discovered that Ira had been driving cattle all day, within others' eyesight. Jack was not in the area at all. It turned out the whole deal was bogus. Campbell remained in jail, "slowly but surely wasting away." His jailers all believed he was innocent.

## I'm Leaving on the Next Train

Mr. and Mrs. William Foley "bid adieu" to Grand Junction on Monday night, January 20, 1890. It was sad news to some citizens in town. The Foleys had recently run a restaurant and rooming house. The "mourners" had been sold meal tickets for the restaurant, and with the couple gone, they were out

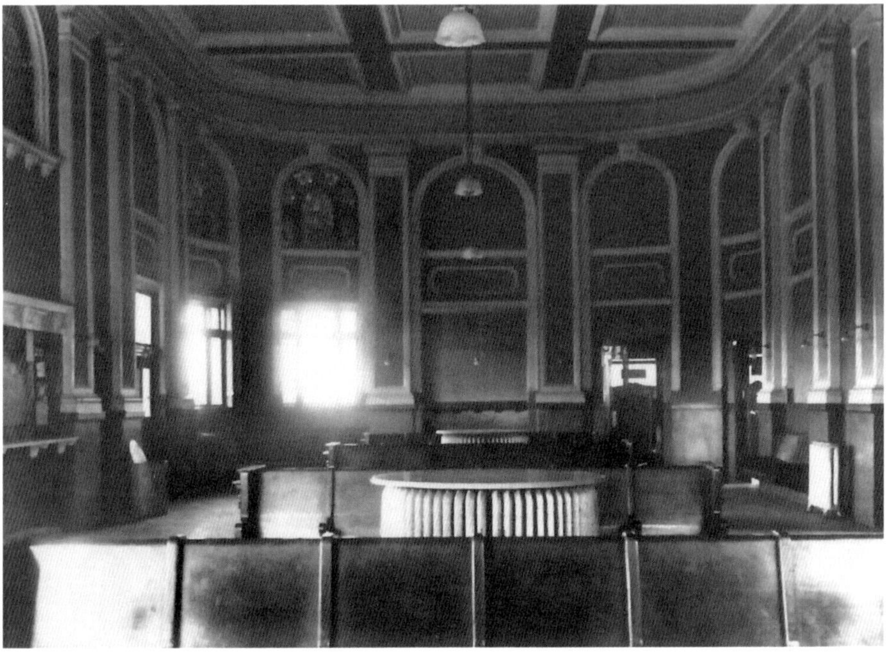

This may be the only picture of the interior of the newly built Union Depot. The Italian Renaissance–style building was designed by Henry J. Schlacks, a noted architect, and constructed in 1905. It replaced the original frame depot from 1882. Though the railroad still debarks from this location, the old station has been abandoned for years, and the inside has deteriorated. *Courtesy of Loyd Files Research Library.*

many a repast. The Foleys weren't picky about whom they pillaged. They may have ultimately been heading to the Klondike gold rush, for they stole a coat and two cloaks from two different dry cleaners.

Fortunately, Sheriff Cramer was on the outgoing train, escorting six "candidates for the state penitentiary." A telegraph to the lawman prompted the arrest of the Foleys, and he was able to collect all the meal monies and the coats. Rather than bringing them back to Grand Junction, the sheriff chose to get the goods and then let the couple proceed on their way. Good riddance, thought the *News*.

Another surprising exodus happened about the same time two years later. William Main was a streetcar driver, and on his route, he collected mail from the various hotels around town. On January 20, 1892, he happened to notice, at the Brunswick Hotel, the clerk place a check into an envelope and lay it on the stack of mail. Main gathered the mail and then extracted the check while on his way to the train depot.

It was endorsed to a Chicago firm, and Main forged its name and then added his own underneath. After banking hours, Mr. Main went into Mr. Strouse's store and bought several items. He paid for them with the endorsed check and even received cash back.

The next day, Strouse deposited his check and later learned that Main had stolen it. By this time, Main had hopped the train and escaped. Investigations revealed that he had just got out of the penitentiary for theft. City Marshal Barton took the train to Salt Lake City to hunt the man down, and at the same time, Main came into Union Depot from Salt Lake City. Assistant Marshal Cummins "gathered him into the fold." At the time, prisoners were being used to build the new state ditch, and the *News* was gleeful in assuring its readers that Main would join them.

## *Chapter 9*

# A Potpourri of Predicaments

### Tramp Trouble

Thomas Williams was the first blacksmith in town, having ridden the first wave of pioneers across the Grand (Colorado) River in 1881. He set up shop, married and had a family, eventually building his dream house south of the railroad, near the river he'd crossed over a decade earlier. He landscaped the area with fruit trees and tended a large garden. On August 24, 1893, his idyllic life fractured when he found four tramps eating his melons. The *News* wrote on August 26:

> *On Thursday afternoon, Thos. Williams who owns a little farm just south of the RR grounds, found four tramps in his melon patch. Of course he was naturally indignant. He objected to having his property stolen which he had worked hard to grow and he said so. He probably said some other things which the fellows did not like and so they all four fell on him and beat him unmercifully. His head and face were a sight to behold. They left him lying in the field and went up to the depot.*

Williams's friends discovered the battered man and found a doctor, while City Marshal Ketchum and several other men searched the town for the hoodlums. They were caught at the depot and, after a little persuasion, confessed to their dastardly deed. They received thirty days in county jail, where they got all the melon they could eat.

Thomas Williams soon recovered from his beating and lived a full life. His beautiful home, which eventually crumbled into a hovel for hobos, was demolished in 2005.

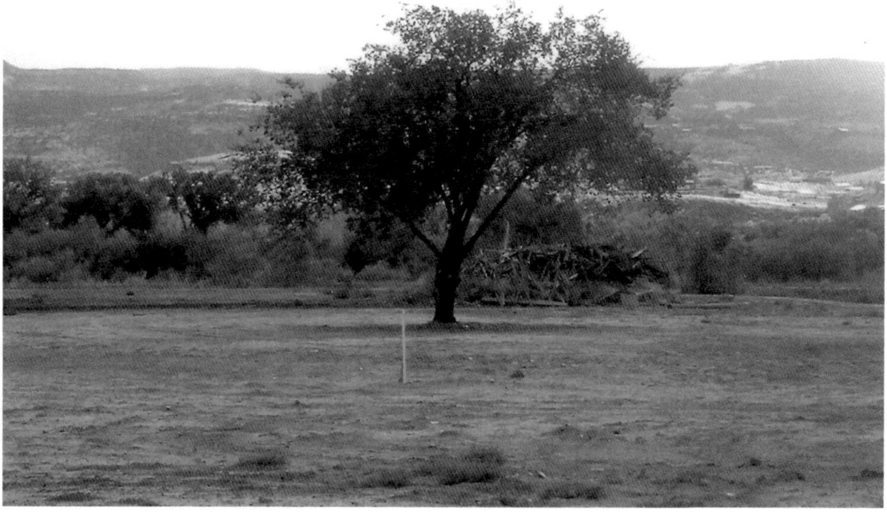

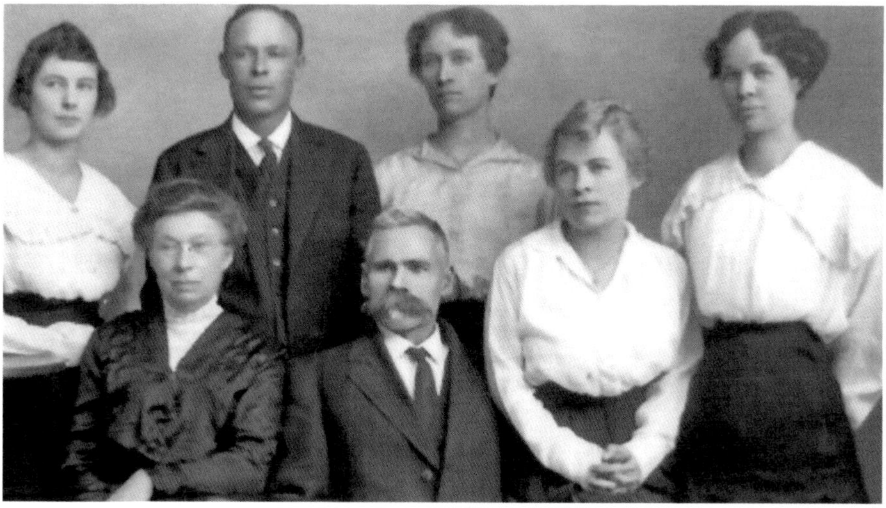

*This page*: Thomas Williams had a temper, and not just with hobos eating his melons. One time, he stopped up an irrigation ditch because someone else was using it when he thought they shouldn't be. For the most part, he stayed out of the news, kept to himself and worked hard. His abandoned home was a historical inspiration for those traveling to Orchard Mesa from Grand Junction until it was torn down in 2005. *Courtesy of Darel Paul.*

# FOUL FOWL

*A Warm Trial in Police Court*
—Grand Junction News, *May 22, 1908*

The reporter for the *News* began his article, "There was an exceedingly aromatic hearing in the police court this morning characterized by mud slinging between neighbors."

Mrs. Barnes, of Crawford Addition (today's Riverside), had been arrested because Mr. and Mrs. Sandie and Mr. Bennett complained she'd left dead chickens and ducks lying around her yard. The "feathered cadavers" stunk up the neighborhood.

During the heated trial, the thrust of the complaint swerved from rotting fowl to accusations that the woman was conducting a "disorderly house." Bennett recounted one night when "carousels were fast and furious." He

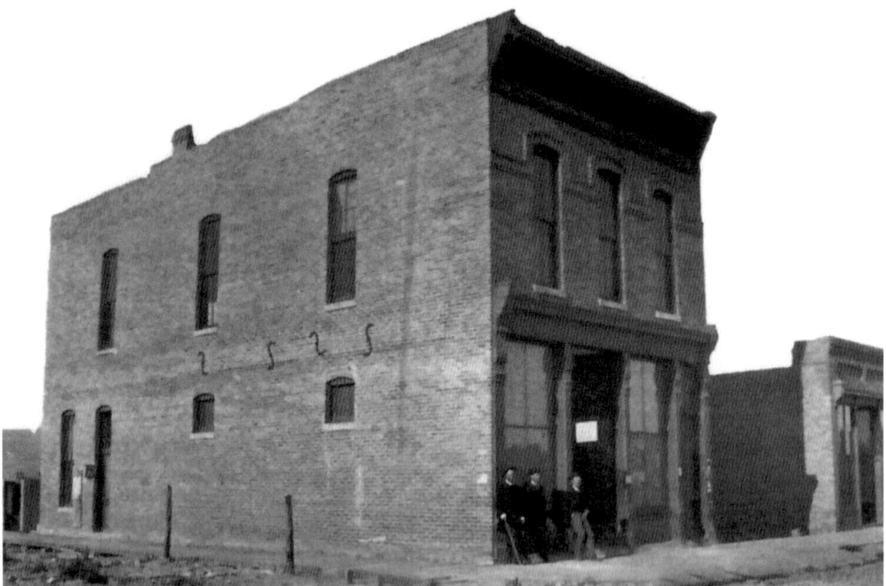

Mandel Hall was the original name of this brick edifice erected in 1883 at the southwest corner of Main and Sixth. It was intended to be an opera and lecture house. Within a few years, the need for town politicians to have a good place to meet caused Mr. Mandel, of New York, to rent out rooms to them. Next, the court moved in, and it remained the courthouse until the mid-1920s. Today it is a bagel shop. *Courtesy of Loyd Files Research Library.*

insinuated that the woman's daughter was a prostitute. He was promptly called a liar by Mrs. Barnes. This earned her a severe reprimand by the court. "The long and searching look that Mrs. Barnes, who is not a bad looking or physically small woman, gave Bennett after he left the witness stand was almost sufficient to melt an average man into his boots," the reporter noted.

Then Mrs. Sandie entered the witness stand and "scorched" Mrs. Barnes "something fierce." She also said, "This woman calls me a Dago. Well, what if I am? I am a Dago and I am proud of it."

When Mrs. Barnes finally had the chance to defend herself, she declared, "I just want to say right here that my mother is a very wealthy woman, and I will give $10,000 to anybody who will prove any man other than a member of my family ever spent a night at my home. Everything Bennett said is a lie!"

The reporter gives a seasoned account of the remainder of the hearing, along with back story for each of the pugilists. Ultimately, the judge fined Mrs. Barnes for her foul fowl.

## A Charavari Interrupted

Banging pots, ringing cowbells and rowdy songs filled the evening air on November 15, 1917. George Nashtoll and his bride, née Miss Ida Wadsworth, had been captured by members of the Bachelor Club, of which until recently George had belonged. They were enjoying the charavari, or shivaree, in their honor. Grand Junction's city band had assembled, and a long queue of people holding banners and noisemakers followed the couple.

They ambled around the downtown area in a horse-drawn rig and had just stopped at the corner of Grand Avenue and Fifth Street. George was asked to give a speech. He stood up and said, "Go and do likewise!" Rather sheepishly, he saluted with his hand, from which dangled a pair of handcuffs. Part of the charavari ritual was to shackle husband and wife together, but Ida had to forgo that bit of the fun when her husband accidentally closed her side of the apparatus before it reached its destination. Then, he accidentally broke off the key.

As George sat down beside Ida, ready for the procession to continue, a bulldog ran up to the rig and leaped, latching onto the poor horse's nose. The noise level increased dramatically as the horse and half a dozen strong men struggled to loosen the beast's hold.

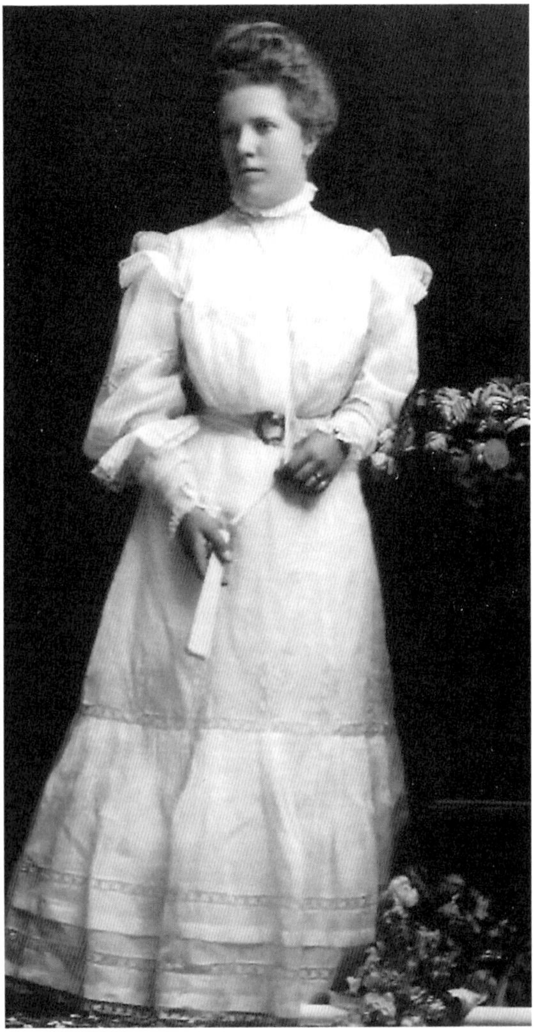

Ida Wadsworth's father owned a grocery store on Main Street and did rather well for his family. The family home still stands at the southwest corner of Gunnison and Fourth Streets. Ida was an early graduate of Grand Junction High School, which was located where the old courthouse is, at Sixth and Rood. *Courtesy of Loyd Files Research Library.*

With all the agitation, the bride and groom were forgotten. They held on tenaciously to the bucking rig until someone saw their plight and helped them onto solid ground. Finally, the dog was removed from the horse, and the bleeding steed was led to the veterinary hospital. The rig was abandoned as the celebrated couple joined the crowd and headed for the Wadsworth home to spend "several hours in jollification."

Eventually, a locksmith came and relieved George of his shackles. With such an inauspicious start to their marriage, it was hoped everything would be downhill from there on.

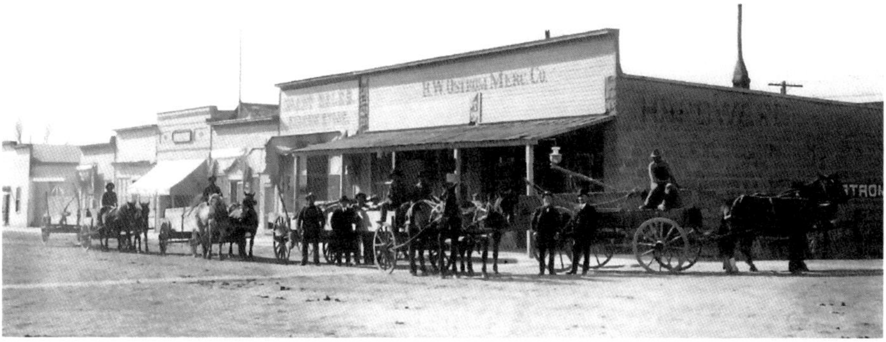


On February 13, 1892, a letter from Secretary of State E.J. Eaton was read and accepted. It was momentous because it changed the name of the town De Beque to Collbran. The town was founded by Dr. W.A.E. De Beque in 1884, so why the name change? It could be the town believed a rumor that he was selling liquor out of his post office. He was also accused of "maliciously" delaying mail. At some time, the name was changed back. *Courtesy of Jim Rudnick.*

## He Had God on His Side

*Twenty-five cowboys who were shooting and rioting in the streets of De beque, a small town near Grand Junction, were arrested by Rev. A.F. Glover, twenty-two years of age, who, covering the men with his revolver, marched the entire party to jail. Friends of the men who were arrested got a warrant for the minister's arrest, charging him with carrying concealed weapons, but Mayor Walker ordered the city marshal not to serve the writ. The trouble started when Abe Ong, a cowboy, called Mayor Walker a liar, and the mayor knocked him down. The cowboys then rode through the streets of the village shooting their revolvers and shouting.*

—Grand Junction Daily Sentinel, *June 12, 1913*

## Meandering Bullet

Mr. and Mrs. Guy Michener and their two children were moving from Casper, Wyoming, to Glenwood Springs. With all their belongings, they'd had to take two trucks. Mother and father led in one truck, while the son, Frank, drove the other. His eleven-year-old sister, Anastasia, sat in the passenger seat. Little did the close family know this trip would change their lives forever.

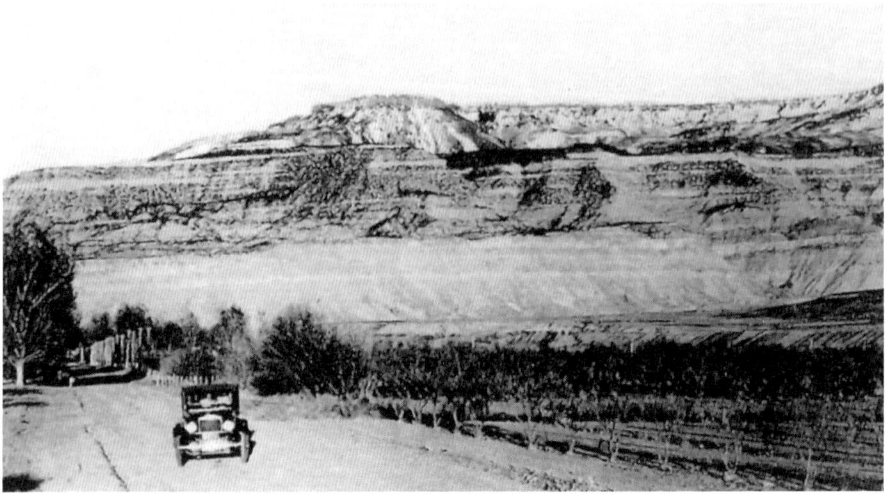

The story of the meandering bullet seems extraordinary and perhaps untrue. A call to Rob Kurtzman, a seasoned Mesa County coroner, confirmed that a bullet could travel the trajectory described in the news article, though it was highly unusual. The Micheners wound up living in Glenwood Springs. *Author's collection.*

It was September 1921, harvest time on the Western Slope. They had just passed through Grand Junction and were meandering toward Palisade, famous for its delectable peaches. Acres and acres of ripened orchards fragranced the air. Anastasia could no longer resist the delicious aroma and asked her brother to stop so she could pick a peach.

Frank noted that their parents were already far ahead of them, but she begged. Two miles east of Clifton, he relented. Frank stopped the truck on the side of the road, near a heavily laden peach tree, and Anastasia bounded out. Her brother grabbed an overhanging branch and shook until a few peaches dropped to the ground. Satisfied, they gathered the fruit and climbed back into the truck.

Somehow, their movements jostled the .22-caliber rifle that hung in the back window, and it came out of its frame. It fell in such a way that a bullet discharged, striking Anastasia below her left knee, and traveled up her body to her left breast, just below her heart.

With an anguished cry, Frank gathered his sister into his arms and headed for a nearby home. The Bosleys tried to stop the flow of blood as Frank ran back to his truck to catch up to his parents. She died within minutes of her parents reaching her.

Though the trajectory of the bullet was highly unusual, the coroner decided no inquest was needed. It had simply been a freak accident.

## A Fire in the Jail

*There was a fire in front of the county jail, Wednesday night, where were found several boxes of burning drugs. It seems that Deputy Sheriff McArthur had gone down town leaving a burning lamp in the front room of the jail. The lamp exploded, catching fire to several boxes of drugs which were stored in the room. The two prisoners who were confined in the jail at once realized their danger and raised the alarm which was heard by Mrs. Hartshorn and several neighbors. Mr. W.S. Sullivan was the first gentleman on the ground, and breaking the door he soon had the burning boxes which were filled with perfume and drugs, in the street and with a bucket of water the fire was soon put out. The danger was all over by the time the crowd was on the ground. But for the timely assistance of Mr. Sullivan and neighbors the fire would have gained such headway that it would have been impossible to save the building or prisoners. The damage is light. Quite a lot of commotion though.*
—Grand Junction News, *October 2, 1886*

## The Judge Fudges

An excited crowd milled along Main Street as the bicyclists prepared for the starting gunshot. It was July 22, 1896. The summer evening held a hint of precipitation—perfect conditions for the eight-or-so-mile race. In a few days, the businessmen would line up and race, but tonight, the professional men were showcasing their mettle.

Bicycling was consuming the minds of Victorian men and women. By 1896, over 150 bicycle factories flourished in the United States, producing one thousand different makes. The Western Slope joined the furor, and Grand Junction had even formed a bicycle club. Two of its own, Alex and Will Struthers, had won multiple awards in regional racing.

This particular event was organized by Samuel G. McMullin, a fine lawyer (who'd one day be murdered, allegedly by his second wife and her lover). Lining up at Fourth and Main were three doctors, a dentist, several lawyers (including McMullin) and even a judge. Jeweler M.L. Roberts was the official timekeeper.

Each participant was given a handicap in order to equalize the race. Judge John L. Gray was awarded the highest, fourteen minutes. At three hundred pounds, some wondered if he could finish such a substantial race. If the judge did any wondering, it didn't show on his face as he mounted his "wheel."

When the shot rang out, he rode off alone at a leisurely pace. Fourteen minutes later, the rest mounted up and headed off in staggered style.

The route coursed along the county road (today's D Road) past the Indian School to the old C.W. Steele orchard at 30 Road, turned north a half mile to D½ Road and then commenced westward, where the race would end at its starting point.

When the cyclists had disappeared in a cloud of dust, men on Main Street began their wagers. The clear favorites were Dr. Warner and attorney Guy Sternberg, both scratch wheelmen. About three-quarters of an hour later, the crowd murmured with astonishment when the first person to pull into sight—was the judge.

Merle McClintock, a young lady and spectator of the race, remarked in a September 26, 1932 *Daily Sentinel* article on how "fresh" the judge looked when he rode in.

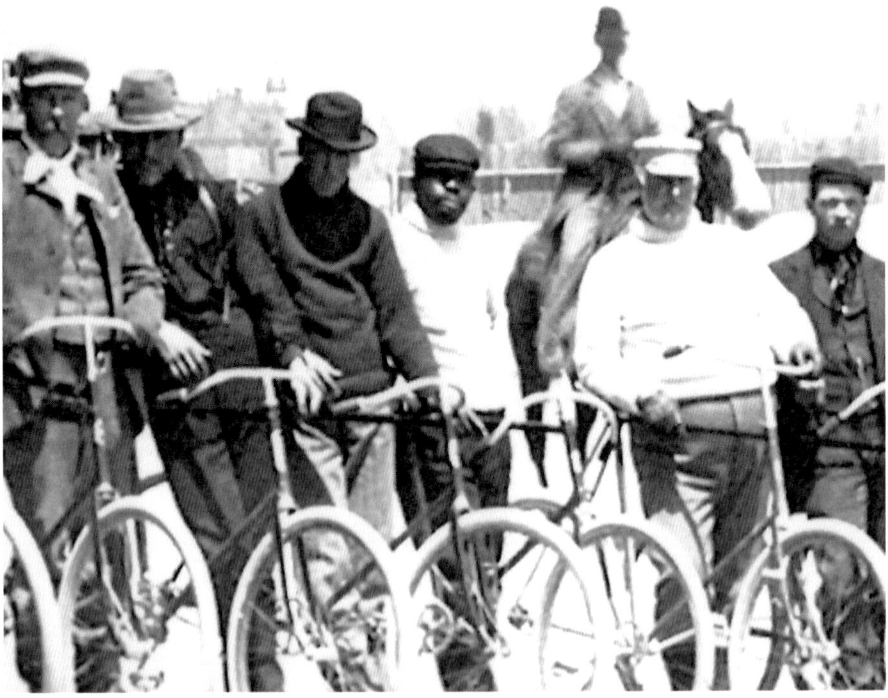

The rather large gent in this lineup is Judge John Gray. He was born in New York in 1841 and brought his family to Colorado in 1883. In 1884, he moved to Montrose. He opened a law office in an adobe shack and hung out his shingle. According to the *Montrose Daily Press*, his first client was a horse thief. For a few years, he lived in Grand Junction, but he eventually moved back to Montrose, where he died at the age of ninety-eight, "leaving a never-ending legacy." *Courtesy of Loyd Files Research Library.*

After all the participants had whizzed, wobbled or walked in, the scores were tallied. That's when timekeeper Roberts discovered that Judge Gray had somehow missed making an appearance at the Steele corner. With a shrug, he told how he'd ridden his bike to Ninth and Main, got off his wheel and hid in the bushes as the other riders raced past. He waited an appropriate time before hopping back on his bike and pedaling triumphantly down Main Street.

The *Grand Junction News* of July 25, 1896, kindly pretended that the "wily fat man" had played a practical joke on his fellow riders. But the citizens weren't so sure.

By 1897, Judge John L. Gray had moved to Meeker, maybe from embarrassment.

## Pistol Packin' Kate

Kate Harlow and her husband, John, were among the first settlers on the Western Slope. John became a judge and the first justice of the peace. They erected several buildings on Main Street and opened a restaurant

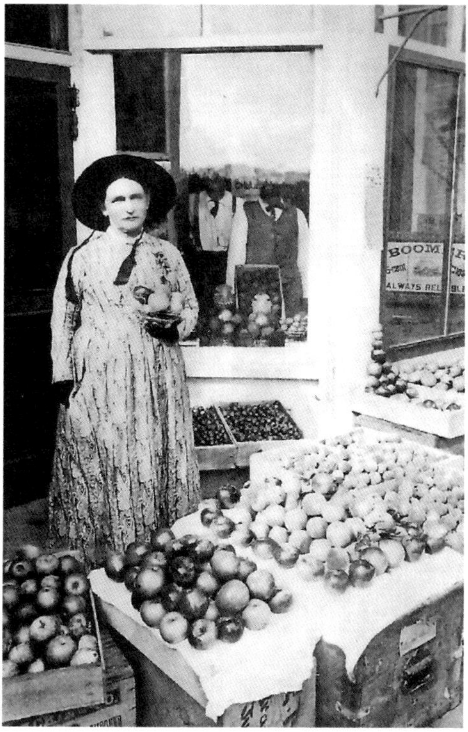

Kate Harlow was married to one of the first judges in Grand Junction, John Petal Harlow. She was mentioned quite often in the *News*, as she brought in delicious samples of fruits and vegetables from their ranch near Palisade. The *News* played no favorites, however, and also mentioned her darker moments. *Courtesy of Loyd Files Research Library.*

at the southeast corner of Main and Fifth. Ranch life called to them, and they eventually moved to the foot of the Grand Mesa, near Palisade, and Peachvale became home.

Kate was suited to the pioneer life, and she was as tough as they came. It was Kate's way or hit the Oregon Trail with you! Tales of spirited encounters with her were told with a shudder. One such story involved the town marshal, a cow and a shotgun.

George Smith was city marshal in 1883. With little going on besides horse thieving, drunkards, a murder here or there and keeping the dust out of his teeth, he didn't need another irritation. So when Kate Harlow's cow got loose, he ran it to the pound. This did not sit well with Kate, who used the milk for her restaurant.

Breakfast had just been served when Marshal Smith sauntered in to inform Kate of the location of her "bossey." He "shot out of the building" mighty fast when Kate grabbed her shotgun and established who really was "bossey."

That wasn't Kate's only tirade. Close to that time, Ed Slocumb incurred her wrath by camping on her beloved Peachvale while he dug a ditch. Somewhat possessive of her land, she looked for an opportunity to explain her feelings to Ed. One evening, he came to eat supper at her restaurant. He, too, became familiar with the business end of Kate's gun.

In 1893, now a widow, Kate was brought before the judge when "things got warlike" at her ranch. She'd leased her fruit farm to Lane & Spencer, and when a misunderstanding muddied the contract, she made threats. Justice Sweney heard the case, and when the prosecution asked for a continuance, it was denied. The case was dismissed, and Kate was released to threaten another day.

## Attack!

The Denver & Rio Grande Railroad had a popular eating house about where Pufferbelly Station Restaurant is today, next to the train depot on Pitkin and Second. In 1911, the chief cook was H. Curtis, a rather big man and tough culinary administrator. In some ways that was very good, as few people got food poisoning at his establishment. It wasn't so good for Jerry Jones, his diminutive and inept dishwasher.

Curtis was "feeling sore at the world" one summer day. He imbibed his and another's share of alcohol and was in "one of those real mean dispositions." The dishwasher picked the wrong day to be halfhearted in his duties, and when his boss noticed a spot of cooked egg left on a plate after Jerry had washed it, he grabbed a butcher knife and chased the man for four blocks.

Up one block and down the other, the petite Jerry eluded his attacker. He was finally able to get a policeman's attention, and Curtis was quickly "jugged" into jail. The cook stood before the judge the next morning and was fined ten dollars plus court costs. As ornery as he was, he found some good soul to borrow the money from.

Early Grand Junction streets were not only dirty and very unpleasant in a rainstorm, but there often were vicious vignettes played out before startled passersby as well. Where William and Louisa Nishwitz were concerned, no one was surprised when, once again, their marital problems spilled out into the streets.

Shortly after lunch on January 7, 1903, the brittle winter air was shattered by Mr. Nishwitz's cries. His wife had chased him out of the Revere rooming house that they owned, and she was pummeling him as he ran. William didn't raise a hand to her or try to stop her blows. By the time they reached Main Street, a crowd of nearly one hundred had gathered, shaking their heads and clicking their teeth. When Justice Byers happened along, he stepped in and stopped the onslaught. Louisa stalked back to the Revere, and William did his best to soften the crowd's ire.

He proclaimed that his wife didn't know what she was doing and that he would never lift a hand to hurt her. Several years later, Louisa visited the insane asylum in Pueblo, where she was treated and released. She was welcomed back by her loving husband.

Humans aren't the only species who attack others. The *Daily Sentinel* reported bird warfare on July 2, 1900:

> *Passersby and bicyclists have been experiencing a strange warfare made upon them by a bird that has its nest in a large tree on the south side of Main Street, near the adobe buildings formerly owned by the Town Company (about where the Avalon Theater is now). This bird when it sees a bicyclist coming on a wheel, makes a dive at the rider and hovers over his or her head, making attempts to strike the person with its wings or peck at them. This has continued for a week past, until wheelmen have become afraid to venture along the path, because they have no use of their arms to any extent and the bird makes no hesitancy of diving right for the face of the individual rider. The bird has young in the tree and is certainly a valiant defender of its brood.*

It was a tale of dog-eat-dog on a February 1893 day. One of the *News* editors caught the whole soap opera and shared with the readers. He'd been walking down Fourth Street toward Main when a small dog romped happily by, a nicely wrapped package of meat clamped in his jaws. Just then, a much larger dog ran up and stole the meat right out of his mouth! The crafty canine zipped away.

> *The young dog, evidently realizing the importance of the case, ran back with an air of the most intense interest. When he reached the corner of Fourth and Main streets, he looked first one way and the other, but not seeing the object of his search, he rushed wildly over to the post office and as the front door was constantly opening and shutting, he flipped in, looked around hastily and still not finding his master, ran out to continue his search on the street.*

The *News* man felt sorry for the little dog, whom it was obvious had been given charge of the family's evening meal to carry home. After he was

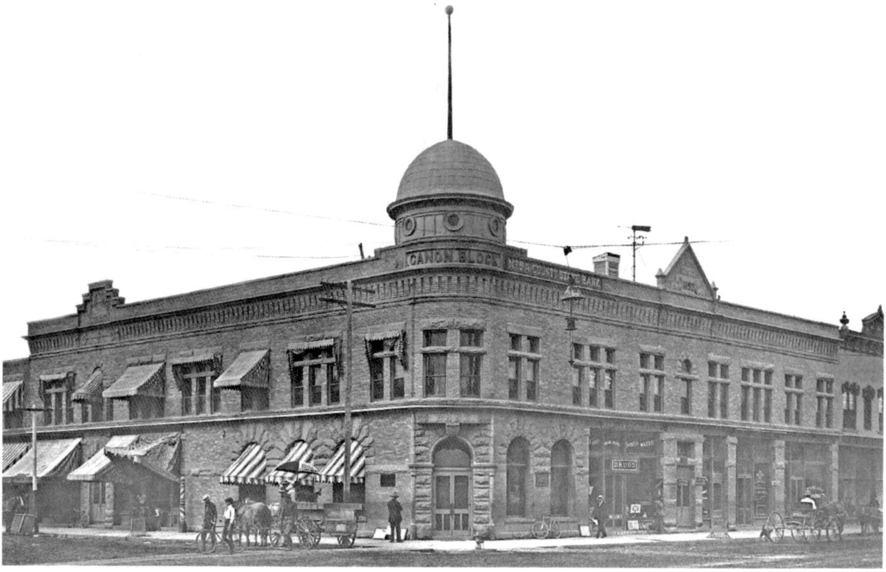


One of the most beautiful buildings in early Grand Junction was the Canon Block, on the southwest corner of Main and Fourth. If you walked down the left side (facing east) away from the corner, you'd shortly be at the post office's entrance. There were more offices and businesses on this one corner than any other in town. *Courtesy of Loyd Files Research Library.*

attacked and robbed, he went looking for his master to explain. The editor hoped the master would not beat the dog. If the master was a subscriber to the *News*, he'd learn what a faithful pup he had.

## As Innocent as Babes

The summer of 1911 was chaotic with crime. About the same time a cook was chasing his dishwasher, Clark A. Wolfkill drowned. Somewhat of an eccentric, he lived in a cabin by the Grand River, a ways east from town. During the summer months, when he bitterly complained of the heat, he was in the habit of swimming several times a week in the river in his underwear.

That's how four children, three of them homeless and another who lived with his devoted mother, made the front page of the newspapers. Virgil Wilson, Gladys Thompson, Lillian Osborne and Lee Baker found Wolfkill submerged in five feet of water on July 12. They knew him. As a matter of fact, he had paid a local restaurant to feed the girls, who were setting up a tent on the river. He'd given them some furniture for it, too.

Suicide, due to the hot weather, was one theory for Wolfkill's death. Another was he'd had an accident and fallen in. People who knew him refuted both of these, but when a third, unthinkable theory presented itself, the public readily accepted it.

The children had done it.

The autopsy and inquest provided insufficient evidence to answer the questions of how and who, but the coroner's jury still found the children guilty. There was motive, they thought. The furniture could have made them greedy. And if Wolfkill often swam in his underclothes after taking his outerwear off at the shore, where were his shoes? Also, in the cabin was found a container of what might be poison. Perhaps the children had gotten rid of their benefactor with it. The questions presented scenarios that couldn't be ignored.

While they awaited a preliminary hearing, the jail was home for the children. Three good meals a day suited them, and they didn't seem to mind the bars. Lee Baker's mother stayed with him at the jail, encouraging him through the bars. She vehemently declared that all the children were "innocent as babes!"

The courtroom had never been so crowded as on the morning of July 24. Justice of the Peace J.H. Hill dismissed the case after only an hour and a half of testimony. A collective sigh ran through the gallery. The children merely smiled as Baker's mother happily cried, "I told you so, Lee."

After ten days in jail, the children were released. Baker said he was going to work to stay out of trouble, but it is unclear what happened to the other three. Without parents, it was thought the authorities would step in and take action on their behalf. Mesa County may have been the first in Colorado to accuse four children of murder.

## COAX OR HOAX?

The question of why anyone would want to coax their way *into* jail, or hoax a mother to deep anguish, or outright lie about a tsunami overtaking the valley is probably better left to the profilers.

"I'm a crook, a thief, and I am sick of it all." These were the extraordinary words Night Patrolman Hermann heard from the mouth of Charles Green one October evening in 1911. Green, of mixed race, proceeded to list just a few of the latest crimes he'd been involved with, which included bootlegging twenty-four quarts of whiskey the week before and robbing a home of jewelry and razors.

Hermann didn't know what to believe, but it was a quiet Sunday night, and Green seemed sincere. He lodged him in the city jail, and Police Chief Burdett Welch politely listened to the rest of the discourse.

"I've been a desperate criminal all my life," Green said. He was afraid if he didn't get his life together, he'd wind up on "the hangman's noose." A long discourse unfolded—of booze, women, burglary and desertion of the army. This last put him in "Algatress" Island, where he simmered for eighteen months. Since then, Green had worked as a cook in every town he'd landed in and even did a stint as driver for the president of the Denver & Rio Grande Railroad, Edward Turner Jeffery, in Denver. In between his legitimate gigs, he robbed, cheated and stole. His colorful story wound him up in Montrose bootlegging and finally arriving in Grand Junction the week before.

On Monday night, Charles Green was singing a different song. He pleaded with Chief Welch, "Say, Chief, I was drunk the other night when I told you all that stuff. I don't want to go to jail. Stripes don't look good on me. Give me a chance to get away from here."

On Tuesday morning (tired of the haranguing?), Chief Welch opened the cell door and said, "Now get out of here. I'll give you today to make yourself very, very scarce around our beautiful little city."

Apparently "John Barleycorn" had loosened Green's tongue, and who knew if what he said was true or not. He claimed he never sold bootleg whiskey; he drank it all himself. The chief stopped trying to figure it out and sent Green on his way. After finding his cached cooking tools by the river, he took off for greener pastures.

The *Daily Sentinel* spent a goodly amount of printer's ink on an article dated April 4, 1930. It tried to explain why it had mistakenly posted a death notice outside its building. The story began when the *Sentinel* received a distressed call from Palisade. Ned Mulvihill, uncle to popular Grand Junction High School senior Joe Mulvihill, said the lad had driven over a cliff in Plateau Canyon and died in the crash.

The reporter who took the call asked some identifying questions, and all seemed in order. The usual procedure for such news was followed, and then the bulletin was posted. The office personnel were shocked when said victim walked into the building about 7:30 p.m., asking what was going on. His priest, Father Nicholas Bertrand, was with him, and they were trying to ascertain the facts. When they'd heard everything, they dashed out to circumvent Joe's mother from getting the news. They missed it by ten minutes, and in those ten minutes a mother's anguish was complete, as was her joy when her boy walked through the door.

As no one could believe someone would lie about such a tragedy, it was surmised that an accident had indeed occurred, but it was a case of mistaken identity. Nope.

The *Sentinel* began a strenuous search for the uncle, who it turned out had not made the phone call. No accident could be found, either. The rest of the article spit fire at the despicable person who'd perpetrated such a hoax.

The *Daily Sentinel* was constantly doling out diatribes in its early days, mostly deserved. Such was the case on Sunday, June 12, 1921. As with other pioneer newspapers, it considered its role of booster to be a high calling. The problem was that the *Denver News* had published a preposterous account of a two-foot wave of water hitting Grand Junction, destituting many. The *Sentinel* printed the entire article, written by a "special correspondent" who was unnamed but local. The story began: "Fifty families have already left their homes and hundreds of others are ready to leave at the explosion of bombs, as a wall of water estimated to be two feet high, is reported to be rushing toward the city."

The correspondent added that another "wall of water" was coursing down the Grand Mesa after the warm summer had "rapidly" melted massive amounts of snow. Panic was appeased when the readers were assured that "bombs will be exploded as an alarm for everyone to turn out."

The local newspapers received hundreds of worried calls from all over the nation, wanting news of their loved ones' safety. The whole experience was despicable to the editor of the *Sentinel*, and he lambasted the malicious reporter in a heavily bordered column placed smack in the middle of the article.

## Hattie's Wild Ride and Other Mortuary Stories

Hattie G. Pearson was one of the first women in the nation to direct her own funeral home. Widowed in Kansas, she and her son moved to Grand Junction around 1905. The only female mortician, she specialized in children and women for twenty years. Accomplished, kindhearted and generous, Hattie was one of only two Western Slope women to make it into the prestigious book *Progressive Women of Colorado*.

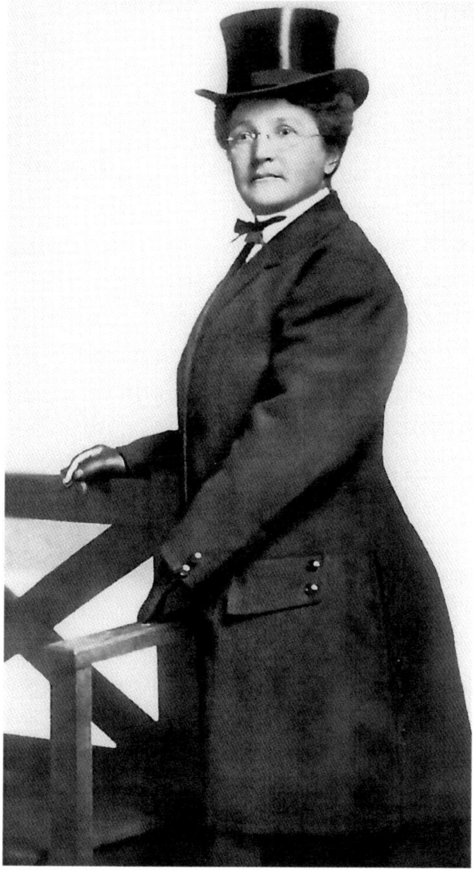

Hattie Pearson closed her shop when she married a car dealer named William Murr. They had an elegant home on Seventh Street, among the elite citizenship. Hattie's beaver hat that she wears in this picture was for sale recently, along with the hatbox and a signed caricature of Hattie riding her buggy. *Courtesy of Loyd Files Research Library.*

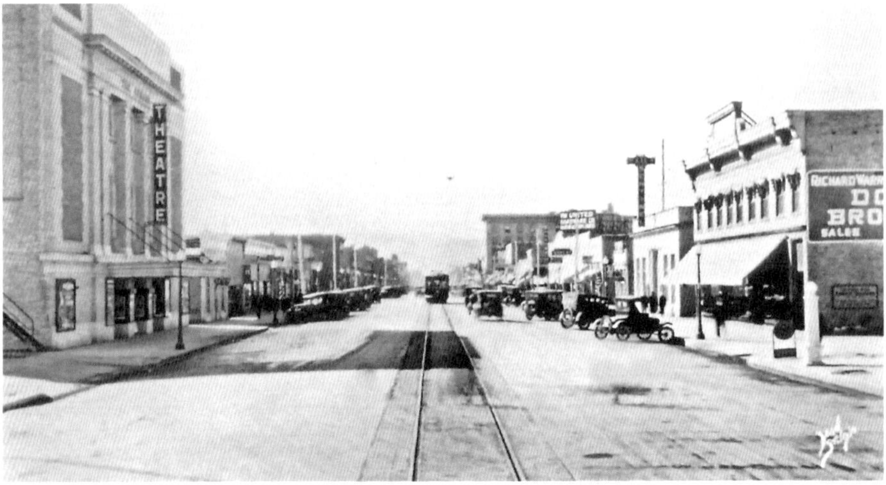


Hattie opened her mortuary in the Centre Block, which eventually became the Lilja Building. She worked for other mortuaries around town before embarking on her own. Her place was located in the front right building. This view is of Main Street looking west from Seventh Street in the early 1920s. The Avalon Theater, newly built, is on the left. *Author's collection.*

Every mortician has his saga, but none compares to the wild ride Hattie took one wintry autumn eve in 1908. Verne Zoflin rode up to the Centre Block, near the northwest corner of Main and Seventh. Dodging snowflakes, he quickly alighted from his horse-drawn buggy and dashed into Hattie's undertaking establishment. With few words, he informed her that a child had died in Whitewater and that her services were needed.

Having no reason to question the legitimacy of the request, she donned her cloak and joined Zoflin in his buggy. Thus began the most insane time Hattie ever endured. The storm picked up speed, and the man whipped his horses to keep up. After he got them going at a fierce rate, he astonished Hattie by pulling out a flask of liquor and taking a long swig. Noticing her look, he said it was to keep warm and offered her a drink. She refused and asked Zoflin to behave himself.

The unfamiliar landscape, covered in snow, flew by. With homes few and far between, Hattie became nervous and asked where they were going. She was told the dead child was a Lurvey and she lay at the family ranch in Whitewater. Hattie knew the Lurveys were decent people and relaxed a little.

When they reached the ranch, Zoflin jumped down from the buggy and ran into the house. Before Hattie could extricate herself from her seat, the man was back. He'd made a mistake, he said. The child was at the home of Lurvey's brother. Off they dashed again.

For hours they rode, snow and wind swirling around their heads. Zoflin emptied his flask. He tried to follow the mountain roads but finally declared they were lost. Hattie despaired until he said he thought they were near a camp. Perhaps they could stay at a cabin. Hattie agreed, hoping there would be someone there she could call a friend.

It was a small miracle that they found the camp and, half frozen, entered one of the cabins. Hattie built a fire and kept vigil over it—and Zoflin, who'd fallen onto the bed in a drunken daze. Hattie didn't sleep for the rest of the night. About three hours later, as the sky lightened, she snuck out and tramped to the closest cabin. Several surprised men looked up from their short stacks when she rushed in. They invited her to sit with them and partake of a pancake while she told her tale.

After she'd "regained her composure," she insisted that one of the men, all of whom were from Grand Junction, take her to the dead child. Still not knowing where it was, she realized she'd have to face the drunk man again. Accompanied by Earl Carson, she found out that Zoflin still believed it was the brother of Lurvey's child.

Hattie and Earl started off on the snow-covered roads to look for the child. All day they wandered, stopping at one home to secure warmer clothes for the lady. Before long, Hattie and the boy realized they were hopelessly lost. The storm had renewed its energies, and the real threat of being frozen to death presented itself. They unhitched the team and made themselves cozy in the buggy by combining body heat and whatever clothing they had.

The next morning, they rejoiced that they were still alive. They were about twenty miles above Whitewater, in deep snow, but they didn't give up. They hitched up the team and continued their quest. As the third horrendous night of Hattie's wild ride approached, the Lurvey home finally came into view.

The Lurveys served the semi-frozen duo a hot meal and prepared rooms for an overnight stay. Over coffee, they learned there simply was no dead child. Why had Zoflin lied to Hattie?

The next day, Hattie was driven to Grand Junction, where she recounted her ordeal to the authorities. Zoflin was found and arrested and could only say that he truly believed there was a dead child at the Lurvey home in Whitewater. Hattie was generous and said she didn't believe the man really meant her any harm.

But from then on, she was very careful not to take rides with strangers.

The life of an early mortician was unlike any other. Dead bodies were their business, no matter what state they were in. Newspapers often reported a body found so decomposed that it fell apart at the touch. It was the mortician's job to gather as much of it together as possible and bury it right where it was found.

The *Grand Junction Weekly News* inserted into one of its February 20, 1914 columns the discovery of a child's coffin stuffed with bones. "The grewsome [*sic*] evidence of a foul murder committed a half dozen years ago was found by Undertaker A.B. Timmerman and his assistant in the Fruita cemetery late yesterday afternoon."

It goes on to say identification was not possible, but the head was crushed and the bones tightly cramped in the box. Coroner R.A. Yunker was sure

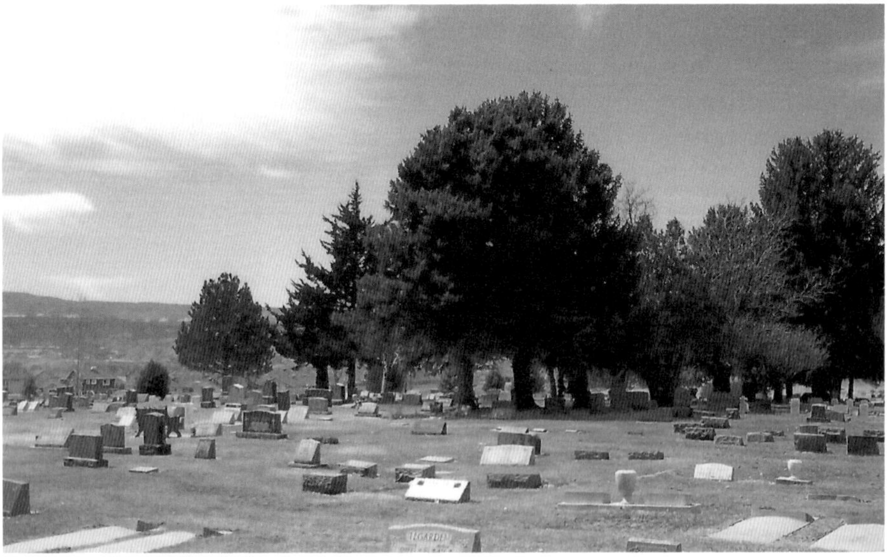

Elmwood Cemetery, at 1175 17¼ Road, in Fruita, is eternal home to William E. Pabor, the founder of Fruita who died after being "stricken with apoplexy" at Denver's Majestic Building. The *Rocky Mountain News* reported his death on August 29, 1911, with glowing words: "Ripe in years…Pabor, pioneer, editor, poet, fruit-raiser, and founder of towns…died in the office of Dr. Hugh L. Taylor…He left his imprint on the state in many ways, and his friends are legion." *Courtesy of Steve Henderson.*

it was the body of a murdered man. The valley was abuzz with speculation and consternation.

A week later, some Fruita pioneers came forward with an enlightening story. Thirty years prior, when Fruita was a "very crude camp," two prospectors came into the outpost on their way to the nearby mountain pass. J.J. Crilly, a schoolteacher from Iowa, and his partner hired Steve Nichols to ferry them across the Grand River. Their pack mules followed in the chilly water. As they progressed, Crilly saw the burdened burros were struggling and jumped in to help them. He "lost his bearings" in deep water and slipped from sight. His partner took off when they reached shore, unconcerned of his friend's demise. The next day, Crilly's body was found, and from the valise that he'd carried on the ferry, the locals learned of his name.

As no cemetery existed in Fruita yet, he was placed in a crude coffin and buried on a vacant piece of land near the Independent Ditch. This land later became the A.J. Dillinger ranch. Dillinger was uneasy with a body residing on his ranch, so Crilly was exhumed and stuffed into a better, though smaller, box. It was reburied in a corner of the new cemetery. The body was again exhumed by Timmerman in 1914 in preparation for another move in the cemetery.

While it is rare for one body to have such a storied—and mobile—existence, at least the valley's citizens could put to eternal rest the mystery of the bones in the box.

The most sensational mortuary story the Western Slope ever experienced began on the morning of December 20, 1913. T.F. Callahan had gotten to his undertaking business at 322 Main Street at nine o'clock that morning. Robert Linn Hughes was already sitting in a chair. He wanted to see a casket, he said, and followed Callahan around to look at them.

He found the perfect one, and when the undertaker turned his back to attend to some small detail, Hughes put a gun to his own neck and fired. He dropped dead on the floor.

Soon, Chief of Police Wallis came running in. He'd been looking for Hughes after his landlady had called him worried that the man was going to kill himself. She'd gotten a letter stating what to do with his remains and property should he perish.

He'd lived in Grand Junction for six years, the past four years at a rooming house at 649 Colorado Avenue. Known for his kind disposition and quiet demeanor, his suicide was shocking to those who knew him. He'd worked for the Union Trading Company before it became insolvent and suffered huge losses, as he'd been one of its biggest investors. He hated that others had suffered, too. It was presumed that financial worries had been his undoing.

He belonged to Hoo Hoo International, an organization for lumbermen, and it took care of his burial.

On a side note, right next door to where the mortuary was, the current Dolce Vita Italian Restaurant has experienced some spooky apparitions. No quiet and kindly man has appeared yet, so maybe Mr. Hughes passed into the great beyond in peace.

One curious event occurred when a "prominent Rood Avenue man" showed up at a mortuary (unnamed) and asked to bury a man in Clifton who was lying dead. He said money was no issue and he'd pay up to $200 for him to do so. He also tried to buy a cemetery plot for the dead man. The mortician thought the whole scenario was highly unorthodox and said he couldn't do it. After the dejected man left, the mortician checked the story out and found the man in question was alive.

The friends of the Rood Avenue gent were nonplussed over his behavior. He had just returned from working a farm for three months in Clifton, and they attributed his strange mission to his mind being affected by the sun.

## STRANGE DOINGS

European occult movements during the latter part of the nineteenth century oozed over into American culture. Around 1890, local newspapers advertised the appearance of occultists at this or that hotel, guaranteeing a wealth of knowledge imparted to patrons. Séances were a favorite parlor entertainment, too.

Books such as Bram Stoker's *Dracula* and *The Picture of Dorian Gray*, by Oscar Wilde, were discussed in book clubs. Even advertising got into the trend. C.P. Bliss entitled his May 13, 1893 ad in the *News*, "Like Magic!" The ad sports a pointed-cap magician drawing smoke out of jars with a wand. Each wisp is shaped into a letter of the word "SUIT." Underneath is written, "They go like magic"

Edwin Price, the editor of the *Grand Junction News*, scorned the hype on May 27, 1893:

> *The rankest, rottenest, bummiest fraud that any community ever tolerated was the manifestations of spirits at the Park Opera House* [on Ute Avenue between Fourth and Fifth Streets] *Thursday night. Why a houseful of people will sit still and permit a pair of frauds to prove them so gullible has long been a mystery to the writer.*
>
> *Spirits are not afraid. There is no occasion for their being hidden in a calico cabinet. Now, if the cabinet were taken away, and then the bells would ring, the tambourines rattle and the fiddles fiddle right in the open light where all eyes could see them while the ringing and rattling and fiddling was going on, there would be something strange about it. But when all must be hidden from sight, it loses its charm and gives a very rank order of suspicion. When once the really live spirit (?) gets into the cabinet, there is not the slightest mystery about the ringing bells, the dancing of tables and the upsetting of buckets. The only mystery there was to the show was—how the spirit (?) kept concealed at the times the cabinet was open. True, the spirit (?) made things hum even while the young lady and one of the committeemen were confined together in the cabinet. But the master of ceremonies had the foresight to blindfold the committeeman.*
>
> *The writer was a spectator to the manifestations of this fraud but about 20 minutes of the last part of the entertainment. In this brief period he three times plainly detected the hand of the spirit (?) while it was poking the tambourines and fiddles out at the wicket in the curtain of the cabinet.*
>
> *The same combinations presents another demonstration of fraud at the opera house tonight. Those who want to be humbugged, should not fail to take it in.*

## IF THE SHOE FITS

Around the corner from Little Italy, on the southeast corner of Second and Colorado, was the New World Restaurant. It had been there for a while, and a pretty waitress named Mrs. Louella Crews worked there. Mrs. Crews was not only pretty, but she was dainty as well. Her hands were dainty, though capable of serving large meals to customers. Her feet were dainty but managed to keep up with trekking back and forth from kitchen to table all day.

It was 1915, so a little bit of the Wild West was still found in Western Slope blood. It wasn't so startling, then, when David Cohen, a cobbler whose store was at 448 Colorado, pulled a six-shooter on Allwyn Lindermann. It was for a good reason, as Lindermann had just brought in a pair of ladies' shoes that he said he'd found in Utah and wanted to sell them. Cohen recognized the shoes because they were so dainty, and as a matter of fact, Mrs. Crews's little boy had just picked them up.

After Officer George Toupaine collared Lindermann, he returned the shoes to the pretty little waitress. Toupaine was feeling magnanimous that day and told the thief he had fifteen minutes to "get out of town." He was seen walking along the tracks, heading east.

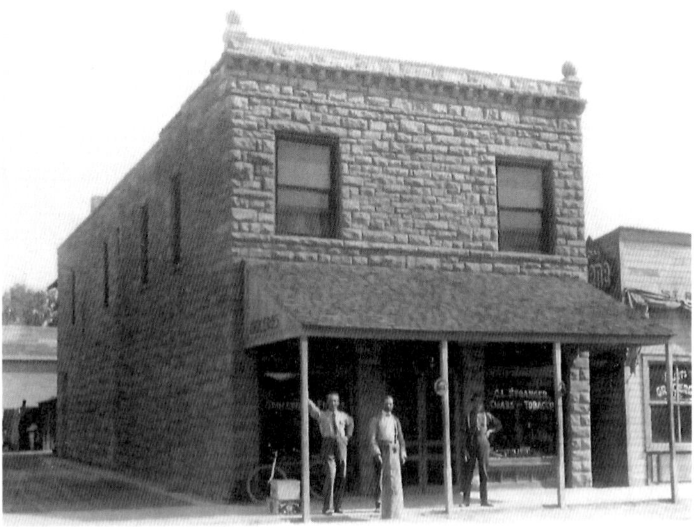

The Strangers were Italians and had several businesses in town. Located around the corner from the New World Restaurant, their grocery store served Little Italy and the railroad employees. The beautiful building still exists, a bit east of Second Street on the north side of Pitkin Avenue. Like so many relics, it's boarded up. *Courtesy of Donna Patton.*

# Epilogue

Dealing with the abasement of humanity can be overwhelming. Like reading the police blotter, it's depressing to see how many ways mankind sticks it to their fellow sojourners. Right about now, it's tempting to act as a cheerleader, pulling a groaning crowd out of a funk after watching their team turn over the football time and again. Our resilience is great, though. A few cheers, and we're ready for the next game, filled with renewed hope that *this time we'll win*. In spite of the dark times, we have learned to appreciate the joys, moments of happiness, smiling faces and laughter that surround us. As the human race, we have done more than survive—we thrive.

# About the Author

D.A. "Debbie" Brockett loves western Colorado history, which is why she writes about it. Having lived off and on in Colorado for thirty-five years, she can't go anywhere in the state without wondering about its stories. Her expertise (and favorite place on earth) is the Western Slope city of Grand Junction.

When she first moved there in 1981, the oil shale boom was in full throttle. Within a year, Exxon left and the region emptied out. Learning about the area's history helped Debbie endure the painful change. As she studied, she was intrigued by long-unsolved murders associated with Grand Junction and wondered if they could be solved with today's technology.

When her three sons had grown, she began her series of "mystoricals" with *Stained Glass Rose*, based on the 1937 murder of Jeanette Morris, who appeared to have been murdered twice in one night. Through research and interviews, she was able to rewrite history with a different ending to Jeanette's tragic story. *Stained Glass Rose* won a 2003 EVVY Award and was recently written into a play by Two Chairs Theater playwright Joe Wilcox.

Her next mystorical was *Our Darling*, which is set in 1924 and is based on a mummified baby found by three brothers in a cave overlooking the Gunnison River in the 1970s. Her research found the parents and told the likely story of how *Our Darling* became entombed in the cave.

Debbie's most recent book, *George Crawford's Attic: Dusting Off Grand Junction, Colorado's Past*, won a 2009 EVVY Award for History. This fun compilation of little-known stories and facts commemorates Grand Junction's 125$^{th}$ anniversary.